Silhouette by Hieronymus Löschenkohl, Vienna, 1785

THE SYMPHONIES OF

MOZART

———

Georges de Saint-Foix

TRANSLATED FROM THE FRENCH BY

Leslie Orrey

DOVER PUBLICATIONS, INC., NEW YORK

DENNIS DOBSON, LONDON

Library of Congress Catalog Card Number: 68-55994

Manufactured in the United States of America

DOVER PUBLICATIONS, INC.
180 Varick Street
New York, N. Y. 10014

Introduction

To SURVEY the different stages of 'symphonic' evolution of Mozart's genius is in fact to survey his artistic
career almost in its entirety. Between the age of eight
and his thirty-second birthday one can easily distinguish
at least a dozen periods of 'symphonic' activity, succeeding one another with only two interruptions. And
what changes can be observed during the course of these
periods! The study of each of these will reveal the degree of seriousness and intensity reached by Mozart in
instrumental composition. Also, his contemporaries considered him first and foremost as a master of instrumental music and were apt to reproach him for treating
the human voice as an instrument of the orchestra. In
France especially, the first critical appreciations saw
Mozart as the composer 'superior on the instrumental
side': bear in mind that his symphonies had in fact been
performed, his chamber music published, in Paris many
years before a single one of his dramatic works had been
staged.

The memory of the boy Mozart is preserved by the
clavier sonatas played with his father or his sister; the
memory of the 'Parisian' Mozart of 1778 is centered
on pieces of a very varied nature for chamber (for example, the *Turkish March*) or concert hall (the 'Paris'

Symphony). Paris had to wait more than twenty years after this date—that is to say, about ten years after Mozart had departed this life—for his first great stage success, a rather baroque amalgam of *Die Zauberflöte* entitled *Les Mystères d'Isis*, to show what he was capable of in the theater (1801). By then his sonatas and symphonies had long been known and admired in France.

In proportion as the performances of Mozart's operas followed one another, leading to the triumphs of the Théâtre Italien, toward the middle of the nineteenth century, the opinion of his first hearers underwent some modification, and his instrumental music—together with the general mass of the instrumental music of this epoch —became quite eclipsed by *Don Giovanni* and *Figaro*. From this moment we enter a period when Mozart was known only by his stage works; when, curiously enough, criticism was apt to adopt the idea that the master's instrumental music was mostly a mere transcription of his operas, serious or comic; a given quartet or symphony became as it were merely an instrumental version of some dramatic scene or ensemble. People were so dazzled by Mozart's operatic work that they tried at all costs to incorporate it in his orchestral and chamber music.

Now, for us, all this music remains absolutely and uniquely instrumental; in all its immense variety one can hardly recognize any precise reminiscence of a theme previously designed for a vocal or theatrical work. As Mozart's theater is one, so equally are his great symphonic and instrumental creations, and neither one serves as a model for the other; it would be perhaps even more reasonable to maintain that the spirit of the symphony permeates the great moments of Mozartian opera, and that Mozart's writing remains always more instrumental than vocal—thus confirming the testimony of those first critics who, as I have said, agreed in recognizing in Mozart a superiority 'on the instrumental side' and a tendency to treat the voice in instrumental fashion. Perhaps, indeed, we can attribute to romanticism, at that time too intrusive, the inclination to see in Mozart's instrumental output only an exact reflection of one or other of his theatrical works. But it must also be said that on the one hand the transcendency of the work of a Beethoven that was gradually being revealed, and on the other hand the tendencies of the romantic school growing daily more audacious, relegated all Mozart's instrumental music, and particularly the symphonies, to the second rank. The latter for all men of taste played in fact an intermediary role, as it were a gradation between the similar compositions of Josef Haydn and those—regarded generally as on a very much higher level—of Beethoven. Up to the present, at least to my knowledge, no special work has been devoted to Mozart's symphonies, nor even to the most celebrated of these.

My keenest wish—though perhaps my ambition has greatly outrun my means—has been to attempt to describe the changing and diverse colors that Mozart's orchestra reflected during the brief life of the master. This orchestra was the constant interpreter of all his dreams; it reveals him to us in the infinite and changeable diversity of his inspiration; it is the permanent witness of all his skill and all the variations of his humor. And it is no exaggeration to maintain that whoever has been able to follow Mozart's orchestral thought, in all its manifestations, will on this account have discerned something of the grand lines of his creative thought.

Then, this examination over, I should like also to try to place Mozart's symphonies historically; that is to say, to show them in relation to those of his contemporaries, and particularly to those of Josef Haydn; this study will form the subject of a final chapter.

My warmest desire is that this little work shall in some measure help to reveal something of what I do not hesitate to describe as the universality of Mozart's genius. This is indeed a quite recent concept. For the most part the richness of this universe in which all the sentiments of the human soul, down to the most subtle, find expression remains unsuspected. And it is hardly conceivable that so long a time should have elapsed before an attempt was made to understand that there was anything in Mozart beyond invariable grace and charming elegance.

List of Illustrations

Contents

Translator's Note

Les Symphonies de Mozart was first published in 1932; since then several important additions to Mozart literature have appeared, notably Einstein's revision of Köchel's catalogue (1937), and three additional volumes of Wyzewa and Saint-Foix's great work (1936, 1939, 1946), which is now complete. In *Letters of Mozart and His Family* (translated and edited by Emily Anderson. Macmillan, 1938; 3 vols.) will be found details of several of Mozart's contemporaries who have been mentioned in the course of the work. Analyses of five symphonies (K.338, 425, 543, 550, and 551) and the 'Haffner' Serenade (K.250) will be found in Tovey's *Essays in Musical Analysis*, Vol. I (Oxford University Press, 1935).

The Symphonies of Mozart

CHAPTER ONE

London (1764–5)
The First Symphonies

SYMPHONY IN E FLAT   SYMPHONY IN B FLAT
SYMPHONY IN D

IT NOW SEEMS CLEAR that Mozart's first 'symphonic' model, under whose influence he happened to be directly placed when he was writing his first symphonies, was not his own father, but a man of incontestable genius (despite his negligence or indolence) whom he met in London as long ago as 1764. I refer to Johann Christian Bach, the youngest son of the great Johann Sebastian, who, born in 1735, had settled in England in the latter part of 1762. This master, who almost at once became his friend, had recently spent several years in Milan as organist at the Cathedral; in Italy he had been a pupil of the celebrated Padre Martini, the famous scholar of Bologna, and his letters to his old master are full of respect and the most deferential admiration. That is to say, Christian Bach was decidedly ranged under the Italian banner, strongly backed by the solid discipline of the Bologna monk; nor could he evade the influence of another man of genius, who headed the great instru-

3

mental school of northern Italy: Giovanni Battista Sammartini.[1] We know that Bach's first symphonies were
based on these two models, and by the time of his arrival
in London he already had a most enviable reputation
founded on the great acclamation accorded these works
throughout musical Europe.

It was therefore a symphony of clearly Italian character that the boy Mozart first came in contact with in
London. Johann Christian Bach, in England, did not
modify his procedure in symphonic writing; he continued to build a veritable overture, in three movements,
elegant and fast, the first movement revealing clear-cut
dualism between its ideas, the two themes being in opposition to each other, the one strong and rhythmic, the
other slighter and cantabile in style. This movement is
generally without a development, and with a single
re-entry of the second subject in the tonic. The slow
movement frequently attains a noble and expressive
beauty, and is followed by a short and rapid finale,
which most often takes the form of a rondo with two
contrasting episodes, with the rondo theme *da capo;* the
support of the musical edifice is supplied essentially by
the two violins, in the Italian fashion, with the wind,
horns and oboes or flutes, coloring the ensemble lightly
and adequately. This form, easy of comprehension, is
marked by a charm both lively and distinguished, and
by an expression of sensual femininity that made a particular appeal to Mozart's intimate nature.

I should add that the encounter in Paris with a great
harpsichordist—or rather, even at this juncture, already

---

[1] Sammartini (*c.* 1700–75), born in Milan, where he was organist at numerous churches. His output was vast and included a
large number of symphonies. (Tr.)

fully 'pianist'—Johann Schobert,[2] also had such an influence on the boy that it was to make itself felt in a field
far removed from that of the great initiator of French
romanticism, that same Johann Schobert! We shall see
the extent of this influence when, after having left
France, he will be called upon to live in a country
where conditions are very different, where taste has
nothing in common with that prevailing in the French
capital.

In London, under the guidance of Johann Christian
Bach, whose elegant clarity he soon began to imitate,
Mozart could not thrust from his mind the memory of
what his father called the 'miserable Schobert,' and in
fact the slow movement of his First Symphony is impregnated with a dull and muttering sadness, quite characteristic of the Silesian master (K.16).

*1

The symphony in question is, I feel convinced, Mozart's first: I am strongly tempted, indeed, to pass over
in silence a Symphony in B flat (K.17):

*2

[2] Johann Schobert (*c.* 1720-67), a prominent figure in the history of the period, though his works are unknown today. He
settled in Paris in 1760. (Tr.)

incomplete in its orchestration and containing the four movements of the classical German symphony. With its persistent march rhythm maintained throughout the whole of the first movement, the very short development, its echo effects in the andante and the finale, and its archaic and somewhat forced character, I am led to believe that this Symphony in B flat is *perhaps* merely one of Leopold Mozart's compositions—the first minuet in particular has the stiffness and poverty of melodic invention that distinguish the Salzburg *maître de chapelle*—that Wolfgang had been made to copy, in the manner of an exercise. The fact is that right up to his return to Vienna in 1767 all his boyish symphonies, without exception, will have but three movements and will conform at all points with Johann Christian Bach's idea of the symphony. Now, here, all the traits proclaim the school of Leopold Mozart, and we can now ask ourselves if we are not faced with one of his recent compositions offered to his son as an initiation task into the symphonic medium. In any case, this Symphony in B flat can scarcely rank as number one in Mozart's symphonic works; as we have seen already, it is unfinished; it is, in fact, an essay in an archaic style that the boy quickly outgrew and to which he never returned.

It must be borne in mind that in a child's work—even granted such genius as we are studying here—it is always permissible to ask, not only what was the model for this or that change of style or expression, but even if the entire work whose detail or manner strikes us is indeed the product of his own inspiration; we must not forget that the great, and the most original, masters have copied in the course of their tutelage; [3] copied, yes, and copied

[3] The young Mozart's exercise books are revelatory in this respect.

perhaps at the order of their teachers. And that is why
we mistrust the above-mentioned Symphony in B flat.
The next symphony in Köchel's catalogue (K.18) is no
less open to suspicion.

Besides the string quartet, to which are added two
horns, a bassoon, and a double bass, this Symphony in
E flat contains two clarinets; and the question of the
first use of these clarinets by the young Mozart has been
the subject of discussion. These instruments were at that
time new to London; two clarinettists had been sent for
from there to take part in a performance of a work by
Johann Christian Bach, *Orione*.[4] Now, I have discovered
that this particular Symphony in E flat—written moreover on the same paper as the exercise of which I have
just spoken—is none other than a symphony by the
German virtuoso and composer Karl Friedrich Abel
(1725-87), published by the latter some years later
in his collection opus 7. Mozart is quite content to
score this piece, which provides us with an example
of straightforward and honest music without the least
spark of genius or even of originality. But this example
is excellent for allowing the boy to learn his trade as a
musician; it would certainly have the effect of putting a
curb on too original tendencies, which musicians imbued with more modern ideas, as for instance Schobert
or Christian Bach, would only have aggravated, without
giving the pupil beforehand the indispensable foundations of a sound and solid technique.

Abel, whose fame at that time equaled that of his col-
laborator Johann Christian Bach, besides being a virtuoso on the viol da gamba was a prolific composer in all
the instrumental forms. He played a prominent part in
London life and, with the help of Bach, was primarily

[4] 1763, at the King's Theatre. (Tr.)

responsible for the initiation of the English public into all styles of music in some important subscription concerts that were to continue right up to the last years of the eighteenth century. Such, then, as well as his own father, were the boy's first and genuine introductions to the art of the symphony.

But if Abel's skill and science had a beneficial influence on the young Mozart, it is quite evident that the scoring of the E flat Symphony aroused no enthusiasm in him, and that he remained entirely under the spell of the charming and much more original art of J. C. Bach, to which his first two true symphonies can be directly linked.

The one in E flat (K.16) was written in London in December 1764 or January 1765. Even from the time of this first symphony he adopts, and indeed exaggerates, all the devices of J. C. Bach: a clear distinction between the two subjects, the one rhythmic, the other more melodic; repetition of phrases; development consisting in the transposition of the first subject into the dominant followed by expressive modulations after the double bar; and a repeat of the second subject only in the tonic for the recapitulation. The andante in C minor has but a single subject: it is a figure stated by basses and oboes, with triplets in the violins, but this outline is invested with an expressiveness so profound and pathetic that one is immediately reminded of the romantic inspiration of Schobert, whose memory is very much alive in the boy's mind. There are andantes of Mozart dating from this period which, with all due allowances, translate the intimate poetry of his own genius with as much intensity and power as the greatest works of his maturity. As for the finale, it is of exactly the same mold as the symphonic finales of Christian Bach or Abel, deriving directly from the last movements of the Italian overtures of these two masters.

*3

The second of the London symphonies, in D (K.19), was written between January and April 1765. It is modeled, exactly, on the first symphony of Christian Bach's opus 3; but, if it can offer us nothing like the pathetic andante of the former and if its character remains on the whole slighter and more brilliant, we must recognize the enormous progress made by Mozart in the handling of an art whose technique he made his own with an astonishing ease and sureness. When at the end of 1765 he had occasion during his stay in Holland to write a new symphony:

*4

it was still the London model that inspired him: perhaps the presence of a little coda at the end of the first movement, perhaps the character of the andante, as of a French *'complainte,'* [5] betray a departure from the man-

[5] *Complainte,* a folk-song on some tragic or pious subject. (Tr.)

ner of Bach. But these are of little importance; it is always with the fluency of Bach that we associate the whole of this Third Symphony of Mozart (K.22).

CHAPTER TWO

Salzburg
and the Arrival in Vienna
(1766–8)

SYMPHONY IN F MAJOR

CASSATION IN B FLAT   SERENADE IN D

A<small>ND NOW WE SEE</small> Mozart back in Germany, apparently taking himself and his work well in hand. He plunges into the study of counterpoint. Contact with the old masters, as well as familiarity with Fux's *Gradus ad Parnassum*, develops and consolidates his knowledge; at the same time there is all around him a new atmosphere, that of his own country, which has a share in making his music fuller and stronger, while at the same time preserving its quiet, penetrating vigor. But despite these factors of musical transformation Mozart remains obstinately attached to practices that his London master had himself never pursued with a like persistency: during the whole of 1767—a year of study and reflection—the characteristic Italianisms of Christian Bach are retained in all his instrumental movements; that is, neither development nor a return

11

of the principal subject in the tonic key. Once one has
penetrated Mozart's mind one can, fairly safely, place
this or that undated composition in this or that period
of his life, for with him the use of a particular procedure is so consistent as to determine almost a period
in his life, after which, like a child, he will abandon it,
to return to it only long afterward or perhaps never.
And this correspondence continues throughout the
whole course of his life.

Immediately on his return to Salzburg the young
Mozart was eager to show his fellow citizens all his
new accomplishments, to demonstrate all the progress
he had made during his grand tour.

He has epitomized them in a curious Symphony in
F major:

*5—K.76.

of which neither the date nor the original manuscript are known to us, but whose style and details
indicate clearly that it was written toward the end
of 1766 or in the first months of 1767. Already this
important composition has four movements, and already it presents the viola parts *divisi*, a characteristic
of his Viennese period; the wind parts also (two oboes,
two bassoons, and two horns) acquire a new importance, especially the bassoons, recalling certain passages
in the Abel symphony previously copied by Mozart in
London. But in it the composer, with an astonishing

tenacity, displays the technique adopted there under the influence of Christian Bach, consisting, as I have already said, in putting the first subject in the dominant, after the repeat bars, and then being content with the return of the second subject only in the principal key. Mozart, in introducing the minuet into the symphony, begins here with a magnificent example: this minuet, welded to the trio, has a breadth and power hitherto unknown; it is derived from his own genius, for the example of such vigorous unisons and such a beautiful finish impels one to question how, by what sudden inspiration, the youthful composer could have attained such a result. And the finale, the principal subject of which evidently derives from a celebrated French dance, the gavotte from Rameau's *Temple de la Gloire*, is also a capital movement, at least equal in importance to the first movement; the form adopted is sonata form, but still without the return of the first subject, and it ends with a longish coda, similar to that which concludes the first movement of the Hague Symphony in B flat (K.22).

During the course of this year, 1767, Mozart was obliged to exercise himself also in the genres bordering on the symphony, genres much esteemed in Salzburg; he wrote, in response to definite commissions, a Cassation (or suite for orchestra), and a symphonic Serenade, which completed his instrumental production. Cassations were little symphonies comprising seven or eight movements intended for the embellishment of court feasts or the family parties of rich burghers, or even as diversions in the solemn meetings of the university; they were occasionally performed in the open air, and displayed a freer, more popular style than symphonies

properly so called, and even than the serenades. The
latter contained a fixed number of movements (five),
and between them was usually played a little concerto
for one solo instrument, or a *concertante* for several
soloists. These pieces were generally played in the eve-
nings, as their name implies. Those scored for wind instruments were played in the open air, before the cafés,
and were little more than dances; the others, the great
symphonic serenades, were intended for one performance only, in exceptional circumstances: great mar-
riages, solemn distributions of prizes at the university,
and so on. Like the cassation, the serenade opened with
a march. In 1767 Mozart, both in the Cassation in B flat [1]
and the Serenade in D—which was published, naturally
without the concerto, in separate parts by Breitkopf
under the title *Sinfonia*—employs all those devices that
we have noticed in his true symphonies, but with a tendency to give a more homely turn to his themes, to
lengthen the repeats of his minuets, to adopt numerous
episodes in his rondos, under the evident influence of
the prevalent customs of Salzburg; also, in response to
the taste of a man who was gradually to acquire an
ascendancy over the boy greater than that of his own
father—a man at times careless and erratic, but who carried enshrined in his soul such poetry that he was the
personification of all the simple and sincere art of Salzburg, perhaps one might even say of south Germany.
This was the younger brother of the illustrious Josef
Haydn, Johann Michael Haydn (1737–1806), *Kapellmeister* of Mozart's native town since 1762.

[1] Saint-Foix gives no Köchel number for this. If it is K.99,
both Köchel and Anderson (*Mozart's Letters*) give the date for
this as 1769. Grove gives 1766–7. (Tr.)

On the route between Vienna and Olmütz the young
Mozart scribbled yet another symphony (K.43), also
in F major:

*6

whose andante turns out to be only a transcription of an
air from his Latin comedy *Apollo et Hyacinthus.*
This, moreover, will be the last time he shows himself
the devoted disciple of Christian Bach. Later he will
turn again to his London master, but now he is on his
way to make contact with the great musical German
city; he is going to storm Vienna, there to breathe a new
air, in surroundings where Haydn already plays an important role. It is there that, without yet fully compre-
hending it, he will experience something of the music
of his glorious elder contemporary, and will hear music
of masters less illustrious but who, unconsciously, will
contribute toward the completion of the structure of
the modern symphony.

CHAPTER THREE

Vienna (1768)

THE YEAR 1768 IS to mark for Wolfgang a time when he will have to put forth a great effort in the triple field of sacred, dramatic, and symphonic music, an effort so enormous that one would scarcely believe his frail constitution capable of withstanding it. Quite apart from two Masses, one of which is now lost, his lieder, and his church music, the score of his opera *La Finta semplice* runs to 558 pages. This score, which despicable intrigues prevented from reaching the stage, was followed by the German operetta *Bastien und Bastienne*, adapted from a French libretto by Favart. Forced to display himself as a composer under these triple aspects, a child twelve years old has never, I am sure, performed a like task.

In the branch of instrumental music two symphonies only had been known until very recently: the one written right at the beginning of his stay in Vienna, which was to serve, some months later, as the overture to *La Finta semplice*, the other dating from December 13, 1768, chock-full of innovations resulting from his stay in Vienna, and which could well be the very first original symphony to spring from Mozart's pen. But a quite recent discovery, by a scholar, M. Fischer, at the monastery of Lambach, has brought to light a symphony of

which only the first measures had been known, noted in
the supplement to Köchel's catalogue.[1] It had been offered to this monastery by Leopold Mozart, on January
4, 1769, probably during a stay made by the two travel-
ers while on their return journey to Salzburg.[2]

At a first glance over the score of this unknown symphony one can judge the progress made by the young
Wolfgang during the first half of his stay in Vienna.
Curiously, while the other two dated symphonies contain the four movements of the classical symphony, this
has three only. It opens with an allegro maestoso (G
major):

*7

An energetic and powerful theme rumbles in the basses
beneath a string tremolo and sustained chords on oboes
and horns; it concludes with a perfect cadence in the
principal key; the second subject is quite short and leads
immediately to the first theme again, in D, on the violins, which in fact dominate the movement; it is considerably extended, and allotted to the basses, with the
violin tremolo persisting; and the first part of the move-

---

[1] See No. 221 of this supplement (doubtful works); it seems to
me quite probable that the symphonies No. 220, 222, and 223,
still unknown today, may belong to this Viennese set: they
would date from the summer of 1768 and would thus complete a
symphonic period more important than one could previously
have supposed.

[2] See *Mozart-Jahrbuch* (Drei-Masken-Verlag, Munich), 1923,
pp. 35–69.

ment ends with an operatic ritornello finishing in the
dominant. After the double bar this preponderant theme
returns even stronger in the bass with a cadence afresh
in the dominant. Then, suddenly, there are fierce unisons, on all four stringed instruments, first on C, then
B flat, leading to a short passage, expressive and modulating. Finally, the rugged theme reappears once more,
first in the violins, then in the basses, concluding with
the same operatic ritornello.

The andante (in C) is a short lied in two parts, stated
by the first violins (*con sordini*), and accompanied by
basses, pizzicato, and horns. The finale, presto (3/8), is
a sonata-form movement with repeat bars, double exposition of the initial subject, followed by unisons and
rapid ritornelli; a curious figure emerges in the second
violins after the double bars, and is followed by new
unisons and a recapitulation closely corresponding to
the exposition.

Mozart's two other dated symphonies attest the revolution provoked in him by Viennese art. Already the
first (K.45),[3] written a month after the one he had
scrawled at Olmütz, is imbued with an entirely new
spirit, and henceforward we find a development provided; the allegro:

*8

with no repeat marks, perfectly justified Mozart's
choice when, some months later, he turned it into the

[3] Saint-Foix gives no Köchel number for these two. (Tr.)

LEOPOLD MOZART Engraving by Jacob Andreas Fridrich, from Leopold Mozart's *Violin-Schule*, published in 1756, the year of Mozart's birth

overture to his *Finta semplice,* after suppressing the
minuet and carrying out various changes indicative of
the progress made under the stimulus of the Viennese
symphonists. The andante, for strings alone, calls to
mind some German comic-opera *arioso,* as does the andante of the symphony recently discovered; and the
same applies to the pastoral character of the minuet and
its trio, in which Mozart repeats all the first part. As for
the finale, it would figure with advantage among Josef
Haydn's early symphonies; and one remains impressed
by its dramatic character.

When, twelve months later, Mozart wrote his other
dated symphony (December 13):

*9

this dramatic expression will be seen to be still broader
and deeper. This symphony (K.48), as much by its
style as by its technique, is truly one of Mozart's original
creations; with its first allegro (3/4), full of contrasts
and originality, furnished this time with a long development, in which we encounter some pathetic modulations, and which no longer shows any influence of the
English symphonies; with its andante, a veritable German lied, interrupted by a most unexpected dramatic
interlude, a song whose simple and active movement
has a very Haydnesque heartiness; with its grand Viennese minuet, of so singular a beauty; with its finale
ecstatic with vitality, ending in a novel pianissimo, we

find ourselves confronted by a work that surely entitles
us to herald the great symphonist—who is to achieve
greatness before having written a single sacred or dramatic masterpiece. But here, besides a purely instrumental ideal such as masters like Josef Haydn, Vanhall,
and others, representing the new classical symphony,
inspired in him—and including perhaps the last repre-
sentative of pre-classical art, the aged, lively, and charming Wagenseil—we must recognize that another element has appeared to enliven his music. We are indebted
to the theater and the drama of Gluck and Hiller for
those sudden interruptions in the musical weft, for those
unexpected and wild effects that so brusquely startle
the listener. Wolfgang must have had experience of the
theater for his *Finta semplice,* or for his one-act opera
Bastien und Bastienne; and whether it was the drama of
Gluck, or French or German comic opera, he was there-
after no longer inspired by the masters of purely instrumental music; or, rather, since the latter themselves suc-
cumbed to the deep and passionate sentiments expressed
by the first 'romantics,' by the trouble and anguish per-
meating all music—how was it possible for the impres-
sionability of Mozart to resist such impulses?

CHAPTER FOUR

Italy (1770–1)

THE FIRST TWO VISITS

O N HIS ARRIVAL IN Italy Mozart's first impression of the 'symphonic' art of that country was principally derived from hearing operatic overtures, performed at concerts as well as in the theater. Such overtures did not emanate from 'symphonists' properly so called, who were, moreover, rare in Italy. The opera composers belonged either to the old school, writing for the most part *opera seria* according to the old Hasse-Jommelli formula, or they had surrendered to the new taste for *opera buffa*, which at that time was accustomed to have a shorter and more compact overture, written often in one movement (Paisiello, Piccinni, Sacchini). This, then, was the sort of thing Mozart encountered on his arrival on Italian soil.

The symphony here, then, is most often an *overture* pure and simple, and nothing need hinder its being played at the opera before the rise of the curtain; the Italians, moreover, delighted to hear it again in the concert hall, where it is fully suited to open or close an 'academy' program; often the three movements will be linked together and played without a break. The short slow movement offers but a brief interruption to the brilliant and varied play of the first allegro and the finale; the themes will often be repeated in the manner of the theater, where they pass from one character to another; the subjects will be clearly differentiated; they will be more numerous than in the Viennese or German symphony, so that the contrasts can be brought out with more clearness. These subjects are apt to be shorter, more precise, and will often give the idea of a juxtaposition rather than an elaboration; they will often be provided with long ritornelli, flowing and brilliant, such as may be found on every page of the operatic aria (or vocal sonata); and if in the course of one of these Italian symphonies we are struck by syllabic repetitions in the themes or by the shakes which round off the theatrical ritornelli, this is but what we should expect from opera. Wind instruments (horns, trumpets, oboes, or flutes) are very busy; they are scarcely independent, but bolster up and sometimes overburden the ensemble. As for the pattern of the movement, the Italian masters adopted impartially the system of development, with a return of the first subject in the principal key; or the absence of development—that is to say, with the main theme repeated in the dominant: in this case the second subject only reappears in the original key. But there is also a simpler system still, in which the movement leads right on to the end without any recapitulation, with the subjects in juxtaposition and, by their character, in opposition to each other. This last system became established more frequently after about 1770; it is not unusual, on the contrary, to find in the finales of these symphonies, also very short and rapid, a return to the initial idea.

Mozart adapted himself readily to this new conception, but he was not to remain faithful to it for long, because within a year of his arrival in Italy he discovered
that despite the preponderant taste for the theater, that
country also possessed a few rare spirits for whom instrumental music surpassed all other music.

Whereas the great majority of the composers of *opera
seria* and *opera buffa* practiced the system I have en-
deavored to describe above, we know for certain that
Mozart, soon after his arrival in Italy, had the provi-
dential opportunity to get to know, first, the work of
the youngest of these instrumental masters and, a few
days later, to meet personally the oldest. At Mantua, in
fact, as early as January 1770, Mozart had to perform,
or probably to accompany, a trio of Boccherini at one
of his concerts; shortly after, in Milan, he was to prove
his worth before the venerable Giovanni Battista Sammartini, soon afterward to become his friend. I must say
at once that the lesson of high and pure poetry instilled
in him by these men was not fully comprehended until
a year or two later. At the time of his first contact with
Italian art these masters still played no part in his music,
while the rest, the musicians of *opera seria* and *buffa*,
are clearly in evidence in the first symphonies that Mozart composed immediately he set foot on Italian soil.

It would be as well, first of all, to point out that the
period of Mozart's stay in Italy, a period so important
from the point of view of his artistic growth, falls into
three sections. The first extends from the beginning of
1770 to the spring of 1771; the second from the summer
of 1771 to the winter of the same year; and the third
from the autumn of 1772 to the spring of the following
year. During the course of these three great epochs of

his life we shall have to notice numerous and profound
modifications in the conception he has formed of the
symphony; now the purely Italian influence will be
modified by contact with his own country, thrice re-
visited; now it will be softened still more when, returning from southern Italy, he again comes to Milan and its
Viennese influences. And on his return to this town for
the last time he will bring from his own country a considerable amount of symphonic 'baggage' which he will
have to combine with new acquisitions, the fruit of his
latest Italian period.

In the first two symphonies (K.97 and 95):

which might be called overtures, to be written on arriving in Italy, Mozart, still faithful to Viennese custom,
retains the minuet before the finale; but his movements
are already worked out on the Italian model. He uses
alternately the new fashion, with a recapitulation in the
principal key, and the old, wherein the first subject is
repeated in the dominant; the rapidity with which the
subjects follow one another, and the almost complete
absence of true developments, betoken in a striking

manner his conversion to his new models; if, in the two Milan symphonies we can still recognize traces of works written by the boyish Mozart in Vienna, in 1768, there is no question of these when he came to write his third symphonic work in Rome (K.81):

*12—K.81.

and to complete his fourth at Bologna (K.84; 1770):

*13

Multiplicity and brilliancy of subjects, absence of minuets, constant repetition of phrases, a much reduced and generally much more homophonic instrumentation— such are the characteristics of his third and fourth symphonies or Italian overtures; this does not mean that the ingenuity of certain details and the grace of the slow movements do not reveal in charming fashion the free evolution of Mozart's genius, adapting itself to the new Italian ideal.

Whereas during the first part of his Italian stay Mozart, busy with his opera *Mitridate*,[1] seems to have been thoroughly absorbed in the theater, it is very noticeable

[1] *Mitridate* (K.87), *opera seria,* produced December 26, 1770, Milan. (Tr.)

that by the end of this first year in Italy his instrumental art assumes a form infinitely more refined. In a Symphony in G major (K.74):

*14

undated, but probably the last to be written before his return to Salzburg (in the spring of 1771), the usual framework of the Italian overture remains the same, with the andante always linked to the first movement; but the care devoted to detail, the delicate inspiration shown in the andante, which one recognizes as a mingling of Sammartini and J. C. Bach, the ravishing originality of the final rondo, with its two violins only, and the intermediate minor section, which they underline with their pizzicati, all indicate a profound change in his symphonic manner—or rather a return to the predominance of his instrumental ideal. And to what should we ascribe the change? Perhaps to frequent performances in the salons of Count Firmian, a Salzburger, it should be noted, then Governor of Milan; or else to the fine and eloquent treasures strewn among the *sinfonie per camera* of Sammartini, just beginning to exert their influence on one who was already no longer a child. Or was it perhaps due to the symphonic compositions of Johann Christian Bach which, written in Milan, had the freedom of that city, and were being played at the same time as those of old Sammartini?

The fact is that from the spring of 1771—remember

that the stay in Bologna during the summer of 1770 had
brought Mozart another encounter, with Padre Martini,
whom no man in Europe equaled in musical science—
Mozart's symphonic work acquired a new relief and
independence. We shall see his Italianism mingling with
the atmosphere of his birthplace, to which, already filled
with the ecstasy of Italy, he returned in March 1771.

It is precisely from this moment that, among varied
influences, Italian or German, the first symptoms of
what is to become in the course of time the real symphonic art of Mozart make their appearance in striking
fashion. It is highly probable that he wrote, either at
Salzburg or at Milan, about a dozen symphonies during
1771, namely, K. 73, 75, 98, 110 (July), 112 (November,
in Milan), supplement 216, the overture to *Ascanio in
Alba*, supplied with a finale for performance as a symphony, and finally numbers 214, 215, 217, and 218 of
Köchel's supplement.[2]

*15—K.73.

*16—K.75.

----

[2] These last symphonies figuring in Breitkopf's Thematic
Catalogue have not been rediscovered.

*17—K.98.

*18—K.110.

*19—K.112.

*20—K. Suppl. 216.

*21 *Ascanio in Alba*, K.111.

All these symphonies are, in general, much more instrumental in style than the first Italian ones; one feels
very clearly that Mozart does not set out to build his

symphonies simply on the pattern then in vogue, but
that in writing a symphony he is embarking on a new
quest, casting the most deliciously varied inventions in
the conventional mold. Sometimes the melodies of his
andantes will be stamped with a personal character of
gravity or of tender playfulness, or they will be extended to give free rein to lyricism of the purest kind;
sometimes he will use German dances or French ga-
vottes in his finales, and he gives some of his minuets a
character so original and so unexpected that one cannot
distinguish between what springs from his own adoles-
cent genius and that which could have been inspired by
the recent creations of Josef Haydn. It seems certain
that some of the symphonies by this master, who from
now on begins to exert a visibly growing influence,
must surely have been known and admired by the
young man. From all these points of view the study of
the symphonies composed by Mozart either at Salzburg
in the spring or in Milan during the summer and autumn
of 1771 acquires a particular interest and attraction for
us; from this moment, in fact, the child is no longer a
child, he becomes a creator, he acquires a power capable
of assimilating the most diverse tendencies; his style is
sometimes Italian, sometimes Austrian or Salzburgian,
but even now we can fully recognize the future instrumental style of Mozart.

We can without difficulty observe traces of a new
spirit in these different symphonies. Whether the recapitulations are exact or abridged or whether the developments are content to be simple transitions, there
are momentary passages of attempts at counterpoint;
one feels a growing firmness in the rhythmic design, and
something like the need for unity between the different

movements; everything becomes freer, more individual, and this individuality not only resists diverse and contradictory tendencies, but asserts itself more and more clearly by an assimilation, a brilliant appropriation, of these. As I shall point out in the course of this study, Mozart's symphonies are *handled* as Italian, but *felt* as German.

CHAPTER FIVE

The Symphonist (1772)

Returning to Salzburg in the last days of 1771, the young man felt tempted to offer his new employer —the Archbishop of Salzburg, Sigismond de Schrattenbach, had just died, and his successor was imbued with very modern ideas—some varied proofs of his musical talent; moreover, Mozart's sixteenth year sees him devoted entirely to symphonic preoccupations and grappling with the gravest æsthetic problems.

The year 1772 is a period of extraordinary maturing for him, so that, from the particular point of view that concerns us here, we can say that Mozart then attained in the domain of symphonic music a grandeur, surpassed later, but never achieved by means of such giant strides. Alas! that we must confess that since Mozart's time, no one has had direct testimony of this; the eight symphonies he wrote between December 1771 and August 1772 were published for the first time in the great Breitkopf edition, but it has not occurred to anybody to perform one,[1] and we are led to believe that only the scores are in existence.

Here are the openings of the first two:

[1] The Paris Symphony Orchestra has recently [before 1932 —Tr.] performed the Symphony in E flat, K.132.

*22—K.114   Salzburg, December 30, 1771

*23—K.124   Salzburg, February 21, 1772

The musical world would be overwhelmed with a combination of admiration and astonishment if these eight symphonies could be revealed today; in them Mozart's instrumental ideal is realized not merely powerfully, but completely. This ideal, it is true, continues faithful to the Italian taste; but the widening of this taste is such as to raise the question whether the young Salzburger has not here given to the genre of the Italian overture a beauty and power never before achieved or even foreseen. With a marvelous clarity, suppleness, and solidarity this German has probed the innermost secrets of the sense and proportions of the Latin *chef-d'œuvre;* he saw how to adapt it, without upsetting its dimensions, to the mold of what was to become the German symphony, with its resources of orchestration, its richness, its profound inner unity. It is true that when he wrote his great Symphony in D, about July 1772, he had a model before him; this was Josef Haydn, the Haydn of 1770 or 1771, a man in the prime of his youthful force and activity, giving primarily the impression of vigor, of heroic spontaneity.

Mozart drank in his music with avidity, but his own temperament added to it an Italian element of poetic beauty, sometimes artless and quiet, sometimes burning and fiery, which allied itself with the often rustic force of his glorious senior. The evidence of this Symphony in D is so arresting that the most frigid commentator could not help being gripped with astonishment. But this one is exceptional; on Mozart's return to Salzburg his mind is still full of Italy, and he sets about producing two short symphonies in C and G:

*24—K.128.

*25—K.129.

suppressing the minuet in order to return fully to his transmontane ideals. We know, moreover, that during 1772 it was the custom at Salzburg for the symphonies of J. C. Bach and Sammartini to be performed at the concerts or 'academies' which took place from five to eleven o'clock.[2]

It was especially these two masters that he glorified and transfigured right up to the moment when, cu-

[2] Eduard Hanslick: *Geschichte des Concertwesens in Wien.*

riously enough, he came to understand the symphonic art of Josef Haydn. One might have thought that his efforts would at first have been directed toward the latter's brother, Michael Haydn, the Salzburger, whose genius seemed to be more nearly allied to his own; but we must expect all manner of surprises in dealing with a mind so versatile and receptive as Mozart's. The fact is that about the end of May 1772 he presents us, after the short symphonies in three movements just mentioned, with what we may boldly call the first of his great symphonies. This is the one in F major (K.130):

*26

It opens with a rhythm destined later to depict the clownish fury of Monostatos, in *Die Zauberflöte*. I wish I could reveal to the reader something of the future horizons that this work heralds, and even achieves; we are here faced with a new world that no pen could describe. A veil torn apart by the unconscious thrust of genius has dropped from the young composer's eyes. The barriers have broken down under the stress of widening and deepening; the whole of the symphony is steeped in the spirit of Italy, but this time it is Mozart alone who displays and bestows the acquired riches; *bizarrerie* and boldness in the minuets, tender delicacy in the andantes, gaiety or whirlwind force in the finales, strength and power in the design. Something of all this we can see, too, in a Symphony in E flat (K.132):

*27

which he perfected in the spring of 1772; and particularly in the last, the astonishingly imaginative and poetic one in A:

*28—K.134.

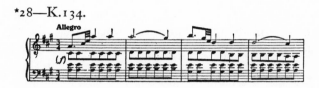

of August of that memorable year. All the musical qualities of his preceding symphonies—the thematic elaboration, the enhanced expressiveness of the recapitulations, the richness due to the use of violas and wind—all are to be found here, with, in addition, the innovation of codas concluding the movements and separated by double bar lines.

Although Haydn's influence manifests itself but transitorily, we can however say that all Mozart's symphonic production in 1772 bears the general mark of a vigor and youthful animation rather similar to those qualities that permeate Haydn's symphonies of 1770. The latter in 1772 [3] had undergone an acute crisis of 'romanticism' whose repercussion Mozart would assuredly have felt had he been acquainted with the works

[3] See in this connection a study by T. de Wyzewa, drawing attention to this crisis and its 'symphonic' importance, in *Revue des Deux-Mondes* (May 15, 1909).

Haydn wrote in 1772; moreover, he himself, at the time of his last visit to Italy, was on the point of being racked by that same fever which, besides the qualities noted here, was to produce those pathetic outbursts, the heavy restlessness, that distinguish the *Sturm und Drang* movement, which, at about this time, was to seize the old world. Heroism, youthful force of Josef Haydn in his symphonic production of 1770–1; heroism, youthful force of Wolfgang Mozart in 1772, his sixteenth year. In this very year he caught up with the older composer —his senior by twenty-four years. But if Josef Haydn's inspiration made itself fully felt only when Mozart wrote his Symphony in D (K.133):

*29

nevertheless he had already appropriated all Haydn's solid vigor and had added to it, under the impulsion of the Italian masters and his own genius, that gift of pure and sovereign poetic beauty which, in truth, belongs to him alone.

As I have said already, it was at the time of his third and last visit to Italy that the young Mozart evinced signs of this romantic 'crisis,' whose initial cause is perforce unknown. It may have been due to his age, to some physiological condition he was faced with; if we do not know of any striking event of this sort in his life,

perhaps we may attempt an explanation of an æsthetic
order, which moreover would be sufficient to account
for a profound change in outlook.

It should be noted that this state of mind seized him
after finishing his *Lucio Silla*,[4] and that this drama is not
wanting in several passionate scenes, set by Mozart with
a truly poignant depth of feeling such as the rest of the
work seemed scarcely capable of inspiring: he is there
content to give the instrumentation a new luxuriousness,
but his heart is not in it; whereas in the graveyard scene
where Giunia, accompanied by a chorus of attendants,
evokes the shade of her father there is an emotion, a
tragic grandeur, which immediately recalls Gluck. One
might ask whether Mozart at some time or other while
in Italy had not had occasion to hear one or other of the
operas of the German master; or perhaps there had
been some old tragic Italian capable of kindling such a
flame in his heart. The fact remains that accents can be
found there which had not previously been heard in his
music. It should be noted that this vein of romanticism
in Mozart is displayed especially in his chamber music;
in particular, the string quartets and sonatas for violin
and piano [5] written in Milan during this last visit to Italy,
with their variety, their high relief, and the depth of the
sentiments expressed, remain the truly incomparable
witness of his first emotional excitement.

In the purely symphonic field the examples are limited
to the overture to *Lucio Silla* and to another Symphony
in C major,

[4] Produced Milan, December 26, 1772. (Tr.)
[5] These have been recently republished under the title *Sonates
romantiques.*

*30—K.96.

whose somber, dramatic, and bold character led Wyzewa to conjecture that it might at first have been intended for the overture to *Lucio Silla.* Without counting also the overture to *Il Sogno di Scipione,* to which Mozart added a brilliant finale to turn it into a symphony independent of the *pièce d'occasion* to which it served as an introduction:

*31—K.126.

The distinguishing mark of the first two is primarily a care for nuance, shown by a veritable profusion of *p, fp, pp, ff,* etc., an unaccustomed procedure with Mozart, serving as a hallmark of this period of his life; next, an inspired grandeur which embraces the movement as a whole and takes cognizance of the tiniest detail. Wyzewa in particular emphasizes the resemblance between the development section of the andante in the overture to *Lucio Silla,* and the style of the big scene in the first act, whose special character of nobility and romanticism I have already commented on; but one is above all struck by the use of the wind instruments, whose blare, punctuating the brilliant and rapid string passages, gives to the whole of this brilliant overture a

proud and heroic quality. And here once more, beneath
the wholly Italian nature of the work, we sense the German master who has just completed the 1772 symphonies, so varied and solid. The same is true to some
extent of that mysterious Symphony in C (K.96), of
whose exact date of composition and intended purpose
we are ignorant; everything here breathes a sort of dramatic solemnity that evidently suggests some theatrical
adventure in a somber key. It is all compact, concise;
and the more concentrated the style, the more direct
and eloquent does the expression become; the andante
especially seems constrained by dint of the effort to be
expressive, and one gets the impression that Mozart is
checking the free development of his melodic genius in
following the bareness of some model unknown to us.
As the symphony contains a long and beautiful minuet
before the finale, we can scarcely suppose that we have
here a work intended for the theater, but the proximity
of the drama *Lucio Silla* may be presumed to be not
without influence on the original conception of this
very mysterious composition.[6]

The general deepening of Mozart's work consequent
on his yielding to the new effects of romanticism cannot be denied; his work, we may be sure, would never
have manifested such expressive power had he remained
in the peaceful atmosphere of his native town. The
worth of his latest acquisitions from Italy is beyond
price. If, returning to Salzburg in the early spring of
1773, we see him reverting readily to the taste of his own
country, there are several compositions that still show
how profoundly the latest Italian 'shock' has disturbed
him. And these works are precisely those symphonies—

[6] K.96—number 157 of our new classification.

or, rather, veritable overtures—constructed of three movements leading into one another, after the fashion of the Italian overture such as Mozart had been hearing while journeying south of the Alps.

Four had been written there, possibly in response to the request of some Milanese patron. The orchestra is that of his *Lucio Silla;* and a single glance over the score of the most remarkable of these four overtures will give the reader an idea of the power of this orchestra and the height of expressive concentration to which it is brought, after the attempts noted above (K.184, in E flat):

*32

The violence of the first movement followed by the infinite despair of the andante (in the minor), and the ardent and joyous rhythms of the finale mark this symphony as something quite apart; romantic exaltation here reaches its climax, and the succeeding overtures have nothing, or hardly anything, comparable to offer. Moreover, a quite recent discovery seems to present curious confirmation of our suppositions in regard to this dramatic prelude.

We know that Mozart, during 1773, had to compose the music for a philosophical drama, *Thamos, König in Ägypten*, libretto by an Austrian official, Baron Gebler. Mozart's contribution was limited to writing some entr'actes and choruses that the librettist had hoped to

entrust to Gluck. The 1773 version is almost unknown
to us, for Mozart, taking up the work again in 1779,
partly remodeled it, and then added a melodrama; it
is in this remodeled form that a German scholar has just
discovered, at Frankfurt, a score of *Thamos*, but under
the title: *Entr'actes et chœurs de Lanassa, par M. le
Maître de Chapelle Mozart*. The music of *Thamos* is
adapted to another libretto, an extract from a French
piece by A. M. Lemierre, *La Veuve de Malabar*, which
had had a great success during the eighteenth century,
and was played in German as *Lanassa*. The author of the
article, Herr Otto Bacher,[7] explains that the first notion
of this transformation came to a friend of Mozart,
Johann Böhm, director of a traveling theatrical troupe,
whom he had known well at Salzburg when the company played there in 1779–80, and with whom Mozart
lodged while passing through Frankfurt in 1790: it
seems certain that he was present at a performance of
Lanassa, and that he had agreed to this transformation of
his *Thamos* as long ago as 1785. Böhm is also the author of the German version of *La Finta giardiniera*. The
two pieces, it appears, maintained their place in the
repertory at Frankfurt and in the Rhineland for a considerable length of time. All this leads up to the question
of the overture to *Lanassa*, for, in contrast to the score
of *Thamos*, which never had one, *Lanassa* did have an
overture, which the author of the article does not seem
to know. Now, judging from the first bars cited by
him, we are faced with none other than our symphony
overture in E flat, which it is particularly curious and
interesting to meet again here! We can well conceive

---

[7] *"Ein Mozartfund,"* Zeitschrift für Musikwissenschaft, January 1926, pp. 226 ff.

that Mozart had never lost sight of it, and chose it to
serve as a prelude to the romantic drama of *Lanassa*—
the German version of that *Veuve de Malabar* who,
unable to endure the loss of her husband, ends by
throwing herself into the flames of an Indian funeral
pyre! Remember, too, that *Thamos* can trace its origin
back to 1773, like the overture in question; who, then,
if not Mozart, could have found it after so long a time,
considering that it had never been published? However
that may be, the choice, probably Mozart's, is significant, and the overture is in every way better adapted
to the disheveled romanticism of the French play, which
is infinitely more alive than the philosophical, or rather
Masonic, lucubrations of Baron Gebler.

The other overtures in the same series, in D, C, and B
flat:

*33—K.181.

*34—K.162.

*35—K.182.

do not offer the interest of the first (Ex.33); they do, however, give an impression of fullness and orchestral vigor which is very striking. Although the form is that of the Italian overture, the working out of this form yields an impression of vigor and solidity productive of complete musical satisfaction. The usage adopted by Mozart for the slow movement at this time (andantino grazioso) agrees very well with the style of these three overtures; and the theme of this andantino has the exquisite fragrance of an oboe melody full of lyrical feeling. Moreover, the first movement of this Overture in D (K.181) promises us tragedy of the same order as the preceding overture; but it is quickly sacrificed, to make way for a working out in which imitations play a larger part than one would expect from the opening. The finale, a sort of quickstep, is not without inducing regret for the rich variety and inexhaustible invention of the rondos of Mozart's last Italian period.

CHAPTER SIX

Vienna and the Return to German
Influences (1773-4)

"THE MUSICAL milieu of Salzburg had sufficed to turn Mozart aside from the Italianism of the preceding years; but it had not the means to substitute a new artistic pattern of a cut to satisfy a genius grown so mature and profound as Mozart's. And under these conditions one can understand the immense import at this juncture for the young Mozart of the visit to what Burney rightly calls "the capital of the musical world," to the city of Vienna, where he was to find an answer to the questions that were troubling him, and a clear indication of the route he was to follow.' [1] Although the Mozarts had stayed in Vienna during the summer season of 1773, that is, in the vacation period, they would have had the opportunity of hearing much instrumental music—the best in the world for stimulating in Wolfgang a renewal of his symphonic art, which is to make itself felt, not during the few months' stay in Vienna, but, in due course, after his return to Salzburg.

The English traveler Burney notes the presence in Vienna during the autumn of 1772—that is, a little be-

[1] T. de Wyzewa and G. de Saint-Foix: *W. A. Mozart,* Vol. II, p. 43.

fore the arrival of Mozart—of so many masters of music
that we can easily imagine how important this visit
would be to the young and enthusiastic musician. 'It will
suffice,' says Burney, 'only to mention the names of
Hasse, Gluck, Gassmann, Wagenseil, Salieri, Hoffmann,
Haydn, Ditters, Vanhall and Huber, who have all
greatly distinguished themselves as composers; the symphonies and quartets of the five last mentioned composers are perhaps among the first full pieces and compositions, for violins, that have ever been produced.' ²
In contact with these works Mozart set about acquiring
a complete professional mastery, which remained with
him all his life. Counterpoint is reawakened in his work
with a new vigor, for Haydn had just written a magnificent set of quartets, several of which ended in fugues;
and the same applies to those, then quite recent, of the
scholar Gassmann, who had been a pupil of the venerable Padre Martini. So we must not be surprised to see
the youth, scarcely arrived in Vienna, dashing off a set
of six string quartets, two of which likewise end with
fugues! But this is not all. The first work he wrote in
Vienna was a grand Serenade, intended for the marriage
of a Salzburg notability, Herr von Andretter; and in
this work we can see Haydn's style reigning supreme.
Mozart has perhaps never written a work in which he so
closely followed the teaching of his illustrious elder.
We must allow that he could not better have chosen his
model from among the remarkable set of composers
then in vogue in Vienna, and from now on the prodigy
of 1762 and 1768 takes up his place among them. 'We
may say that from the summer of 1773 until his arrival

² Burney: *The Present State of Music in France and Germany*,
Vol. I, p. 364. (Tr.)

in Mannheim, toward the end of 1777, Mozart, in short, remains a true composer of the Viennese school.' [3]

It is impossible, then, to overemphasize the importance to Mozart of the lessons learned in Vienna. It is clearly in Vienna that he became acquainted with Haydn's symphonies of 1772, which, with or without such characteristic titles as *"La Passione"* or "The Farewell" or the *Symphonie funèbre,* all reflect the intense crisis of romanticism Haydn went through in that year; to these must be added several symphonies of Vanhall, an artist of similar temperament though unequal inspiration. On the other hand, such masters as Gassmann and Ditters, smitten by *opera buffa,* are in process of creating a Viennese instrumental style that, light and lively, is to have the sharpest reaction on Mozart.

After Vienna, then, we shall see his developments lengthening, his codas becoming weighty résumés of his first movements and finales, the finales themselves rivaling the first movements in importance and assuming the sonata form; in a word, a more elaborate workmanship, a language more clearly symphonic, a more pronounced breadth given to all his instrumental compositions. As almost always happens with Mozart, this serious style is not going to last very long, for *'la galanterie'* is about to overrun the whole of music. But we can say that Mozart in his symphonies of 1773–4 has reached the end of a period, and that after it he will not do better, but different things.

Afterward there will be Mannheim, and Paris; his orchestral masses will be more powerful, the horizon will be wider; but, for all that, something of great intimacy and charm will have disappeared; the subtle perfume of

[3] Wyzewa and Saint-Foix, op. cit., Vol. II, p. 45.

Vienna, combined with the Italian flavor, will have vanished. Mozart's incomparable youth, as evidenced in his 1773–4 symphonies (though, alas, too rarely experienced), will be over.

Did Mozart, on reaching Vienna, intend to complete the set of Italian overtures written on his return from Milan? This is not unlikely, for a Sinfonia in G major (K.199):

*36

with the andantino grazioso typical of this set, fits absolutely into the framework of these overtures. But at the same time this curious instrumental piece, brilliant and Italian in style at first, shows such peculiarly Viennese qualities that we have at times the impression of hearing echoes of the orchestra of Johann Strauss. Rhythms of Viennese dances follow one another in all three movements and—a significant point—the finale opens with a sort of *fugato* that soon takes on a waltz rhythm; decidedly we are in Vienna. The Austrian masters of the eighteenth century saw nothing incongruous in this mixture of styles; examples could be cited from Michael Haydn, and probably from many more we do not know! What is one to make of the finale of the first of Mozart's great quartets (that in G), dedicated to Josef Haydn? What of this fugue interspersed with such lively and gay refrains?

Thus, in the great symphonies composed by Mozart

in the latter part of 1773 and during the spring of the following year, we shall come across echoes of that humor whose extreme subtlety is to be found in the almost contemporary *La Finta giardiniera.* These symphonies, four in number, certainly count among Mozart's grandest; and it is a matter for regret that, following these, he should have abandoned that high ideal of great music which filled him at the time, in order to turn toward '*la galanterie*'—ravishing, no doubt, but in which one feels a secret shrinking from all that broadens and deepens music.

What is the impulse behind the birth of these four grand symphonies? One can see in them a sort of 'sublimation' of the compositions of the two Haydns—for, since his return to Salzburg Mozart felt himself more and more attracted by the work of his confrere and friend Michael Haydn, whom of course he very quickly surpassed in originality and intensity of expression. Mozart was indebted to Michael Haydn for that ideal poetic beauty of certain of the andantes, a kind of reverie that often attained the summit of his artistic creation. For Michael Haydn, despite his native indolence, had the soul of a poet, which revealed itself, not only in some admirable sacred music, but also in his symphonies and chamber music, by melodies of an infinite tenderness, and dances of a quality and harmonization intimately 'Mozartian.' Haydn's career, unfolding itself side by side with Mozart's, in the same town and the same procession, gave the latter the benefits of a quasi-providential teaching and friendship.

But quite certainly we shall come across nothing in his symphonic production that is the equivalent of these four symphonies of Mozart. Never, simply from the

harmonic point of view, could he have written the opening bars of the Symphony in A (K.201), in particular—
a symphony that may be considered one of Mozart's
most characteristic instrumental masterpieces, one in
which he is already completely himself:

*37

and as for the Symphony in G minor (K.183):

*38

it is already such a promise of the famous masterpiece of
1788 that we can look for explanation only to the young
man's genius. The fire he kindled there burned only in
his own soul. Granted, the full working-out of such
thoughts is not yet perfect, and cannot be; in the andante, for example, there is a second subject that has no
affinity with the first, and whose banality offends us,
and in the first movement we are conscious of some
voids. But that startling and breathless opening, followed by one of the most arresting themes of the *Don
Giovanni* overture, that wild coda and the sinister drum
roll to end it, whence do all these arise if not from the
very depths of Mozart's soul?

And if now we examine the first of these four symphonies, that in C (K.200):

*39

with its heroic grace, and its minuet, worthy of Mozart's grandest creations, we shall have the satisfaction of studying a work that foreshadows its successors, while losing nothing from their proximity. Perhaps, on the whole, the slow movements of these symphonies do not quite reach the level of the other movements, but the essential fact is that there is nothing that really impairs the works. It must, however, be admitted that the last, in D (K.202):

*40

despite the cleverness of its scoring, does not quite belong to the same class. It dates from May 5, 1774, and Mozart's thoughts and feelings have already changed.[4] The emphasis now is on entertainment, and the 'galante' symphony has no other object. With the exception of one or two overtures he will write only *divertissements* and serenades, until the moment when he finds himself,

[4] Wyzewa and Saint-Foix, op. cit., Vol. II, p. 141.

in Mannheim and Paris, in fresh contact with a great
symphonic school.

In this Symphony in D the themes follow one another but are never unified, although, speaking generally, their fellows in the preceding symphonies achieve
that profound unity which Mozart, in his great creative
periods, always strove to attain. Although we must regret this changed outlook, it is a sign of the times: the
invasion of the 'galant' style is also obvious, and quite as
noticeable, in the work of Josef Haydn. His symphonies
entitled 'The Schoolmaster,' 'Imperial,' and 'Fire,' in
which we can detect no traces of the great works of his
romantic inspiration of 1772, do, in fact, date from
1774. The Esterház master, more lively and nervous
than ever, had sacrificed his old ideals entirely for the
new '*galanterie*.' And in his Symphony in D Mozart
follows the same path; we can easily recognize, in the
short and delightful andantino, some of the significant
chromaticisms of the astonishing Symphony in A
(K.201); but the unexpected and rather vulgar buffoonery of the finale, despite an originality that approaches
the grotesque fury of Osmin in *Die Entführung aus dem
Serail*, cannot make up for all we admired with such
good cause in the preceding finales.

Such are the thrilling symphonies with which the
'great creative period' of Mozart's life closes; their
scope is greater than any of the works we have noticed
so far. The lessons learned in Vienna, the daily intercourse with a master of the caliber of Michael Haydn,
the deeper and deeper understanding of the works of
the latter's elder brother, and even of those of the other
Viennese symphonists—all this was consummated in
these four works which, at each new reading, provoke

our astonishment and admiration; to these elements we
must add the extraordinary maturing of his genius. I
very much doubt if any youth, on completing his eighteenth year, has ever shown an equal effort or produced
comparable beauty.

CHAPTER SEVEN

La Galanterie *(1775)*

As I HAVE ALREADY said, Mozart, for four successive years, entirely abandoned the great classical ideal and yielded to a lighter, more worldly art, more in keeping with the 'galant' taste which had at that time possessed the world of music. It is now a question of amusement rather than emotion. His style on the whole remains what it was, but the inspiration is slenderer, its import less. The slow movements alone—and perhaps, curiously enough, more often than in the past—will give rise to some admirably poetic reveries, infinitely surpassing the charming but unvarying gaiety of the other movements. If Mozart's present 'galant' period does not permit a symphony, we cannot pass over in silence the various orchestral serenades—bulky ensembles clearly allied to the symphonic genre—which are spread over the period between 1774 and 1778.

Every summer, for wedding or anniversary feasts at the houses of the rich burghers of Salzburg, Mozart had to write one or two of these serenades, consisting of five usually very long and brilliant movements, besides a violin concerto, which was always interpolated. The prevailing mood of these serenades is decidedly the *'concertante'* style; the principal performers are given the opportunity for the display of a certain degree of

virtuosity, which, however, is kept within reasonable
bounds and as a result never runs the risk of destroying
the purely musical interest of the work. But it is none
the less true that these serenades, being occasional pieces,
are more superficial than the symphony proper, and
thus closely correspond to the 'galant' ideal; so it is quite
natural to find Mozart, between 1773 and 1776, occupied in midsummer in dazzling his fellow citizens
with vast symphonic serenades, full at the same time of
that Austro-Hungarian good humor (*Gemütlichkeit*)
and of solemnity—festive music interrupted by incomparable minuets or by melodies imprinted, or rather impregnated, with tenderness and supernatural grace. And
in these serenades there is such a wealth of felicitous
scoring, of dialogues between the *concertante* instruments, such a variety of sentiments (more marked perhaps than in the symphonies), that one is just astonished to see so much learning bestowed on works that,
after all, were intended only for the occasion of some
anniversary or festival.

Speaking generally, the new attitude is revealed in
these serenades by very distinct subjects, by short and
rapid imitations, by exactitude of recapitulation, and by
a curtailment of the codas, lately so beautiful, which
now become (except in certain of the andantes) no more
than unpretentious little stretti. It was customary for
the serenade to open with a march in which, in general,
the first part never reappeared in the recapitulation;
with Mozart the initial rhythm of the march was often
recalled in the first allegro, thus giving a noticeable
unity to the whole. But on the whole there was no
elaboration, no really extended working out; the variety and freshness of the themes replaced the cohesion

we so admired in the symphonies of preceding periods. Here, in music full of fire and brilliance, Mozart seems to concentrate his attention on the andantes, whose beautiful melodies and poetic expression compensate for the too rudimentary nature of the other movements.

In the year 1775 in particular this taste for *divertimenti* and serenades is evident on almost every page Mozart wrote. The opera he had to compose in the spring of this year was itself a pastoral serenade, *Il Rè pastore,* on a famous libretto by Metastasio. Its overture, in one movement, is to serve as the prototype of the great operatic overtures of his maturity; but, being written in 1775, it, very curiously, could not avoid being transformed into a serenade! Mozart is content to transfer the first air of the opera to the oboe, and to add a grand finale which is one of the most lively and witty rondos he has ever produced:

*41—K.102.

The theme is a sort of French *contredanse,* with all the minor intermediary sections intentionally omitted, as too contrary to the prevailing 'galant' ideals. But the animation of this finale and the ingenious return to its initial theme invest this work with a quite peculiar charm and give it an importance that totally escaped Mozart's first biographers, who wrongly attributed it to a period before 1770. In order that the scheme of the serenade might be complete, Mozart, on August 20, 1775, wrote

a superb March in C major, opening with a bold unison
à la française which, obviously, was intended for the
opening of this curious pastoral *divertimento* (K.214):

*42

It should be added here that the presence of a French
contredanse gives rise to the supposition that Mozart
must have had at hand some collections of French
dances at about this time, which were not without their
effect on him. In fact, he used several of them in the
finales of his contemporary violin concertos; and this
practice could have been suggested to him not only by
these collections but by the violinists of the French
school, who were even then addicted to the concerto
'on well-known airs.'
    We have no doubt that Mozart was acquainted with
the works of several of the most remarkable representa-
tives of the French violin school; neither Gaviniès nor,
notably, Le Duc nor Guénin [1] were unknown. Among
the concertos of these last two artists there are some
striking, even disconcerting 'Mozartisms,' which prove
the role played by the great French school in Mozart's
conception of the violin concerto. We shall have moreover in a short time to consider the importance of this
role in the domain of the symphony proper.

    [1] P. Gaviniès, 1726–1800. Marie A. Guénin, 1744–1819. Simon
Le Duc, 1748–77. Grove gives some details of their lives. (Tr.)

CHAPTER EIGHT

The Haffner Music (July 1776)

THE TWENTIETH YEAR

*43

THIS serenade (K.250), composed by Mozart in the middle of his twentieth year—that is to say, in the full flower of his musical inspiration, for this year, 1776, sees the full blossoming of his rarest gifts of music and poetry—this serenade marks for us the climax, not to say the apotheosis, of the period I have designated as 'galant.' It is the successor of the serenades of 1773, 1774, and 1775, but with what a difference! Its exceptional length is perhaps due to the solemnity of Elisabeth Haffner's wedding (she was the daughter of the Burgomaster of Salzburg); but it is certain that on this particular day the young master was bent on making a great impression and spreading out before his fellow citizens all the richness his genius was able to produce. It is really, in every sense of the word, a musical *feast*, in which Mozart gives free rein to his fancy, creating al-

57

most new forms; where, too, rhythms to be used later in his *Don Giovanni* make their appearance before our delighted eyes. So that the late Burgomaster's salon becomes as it were the antechamber of the philandering nobleman bent on some new and ephemeral conquest.

Within the limits of 'galant' music, since all idea of depth and severity is banished from the musical scene, since all is effectiveness and brilliance, it seems scarcely possible to go further; not that, on the other hand, emotions at once attractive and tender are not occasionally revealed (in the long andante, a concession to the Salzburgers' taste for prolixity), or a development of the most highly lyrical kind (in the other andante, in the concerto). All this—the abnormal length of the movements, their variety, their brilliance, the elaboration of detail entrusted to a big orchestra—all this almost compels the adoption of the new 'galant' ideal; but, on reflection, one feels all the same, both in the first movement and in the allegro assai, the great hunting song with which the serenade concludes, how different is such a work from, for example, one of the symphonies written by Mozart a year or two earlier. Despite all the attractiveness—which is great—of this musical feast, this copious banquet, one cannot conceal the weakness of certain movements, the inordinate *longueur* of the rondo, in G, and also of the finale. And one begins to regret the high artistic endeavor which endears the former symphonies to us, even though these may have nothing in them to equal the two amazing minuets of the Haffner Serenade, in which Mozart, with an unmatched maturity, anticipates the ballroom scene in *Don Giovanni*.

In the period we are studying, the young master, as

I have shown, gives free rein to the virtuosity of his
soloists, and writes concertos for most of the instruments of the orchestra calculated to show off their qualities to the best advantage—but never allowing mere
brilliance to cramp the inspiration of the moment. This
virtuosity, too, is ranged over a wide field; he does not
content himself with opposing one performer to the
orchestral mass, but divides the orchestra itself into several groups and makes them 'concert' among themselves. On the other hand, he is fond of using an 'echo'
device, probably taking the idea from some model unknown to us; that is to say, he will write a phrase more
or less long, given out by a quarter of the performers,
the remainder finishing it or repeating it as an echo. But
the repetition may only be partial, or even confined to
quite a few bars, or the end of the phrase, or even its
very last note; but always with particular care that this
repetition is, like an echo, an exact textual reproduction
of the preceding. This echo device, moreover, was practiced by eighteenth-century masters such as Haydn and
Johann Christian Bach; the former specified that the
echo ought to be played in *separate rooms*, but this
pleasantry appertained rather, I think, to chamber music. In his symphonies for two orchestras, on the other
hand, Johann Christian Bach, in the spacious rooms of
the London Pantheon, used two orchestral masses re-
sponding to each other. Mozart in his *Serenata notturna*
(K.239—N.C.242):

*44

—which is itself not strictly an echo—uses two small orchestras, one formed of two principal violins, viola, and double bass, the other of two violins, a second viola, cello, and drums. The idea here is, evidently, a dialogue exchanged between two small orchestras placed some distance from each other, as for example at each end of a room; and one can easily see that if the echo procedure is not consistent, it is employed very wittily. The other composition of the same genre is, on the contrary, a veritable 'echo,' entitled *Notturno* (K.286—N.C. 283):

*45

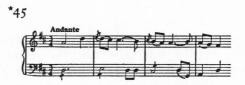

written for four orchestras, each of two violins, viola, two horns, and bass. As with the first, we do not know the occasion for which it was composed. The echo device is used with remarkable understanding of its effects; thus, the fine andante with which the work opens has a first subject of four bars repeated in its entirety by the 'first echo,' after which the other orchestras take up fragments only, getting shorter and shorter.

Sometimes, to give the effect of a more distant echo, the reply is reproduced only after a period of silence; sometimes, again, in a stretto the repetitions appear, first at a bar's interval, then a beat apart, then two beats, in canon; and thus we see the final perfection bestowed by Mozart on a phenomenon of nature known to us all.

In the sequence of his symphonies, which we shall

see growing in nobility and beauty, all these serenades and *divertimenti* sound a note of 'galant' variety illustrating the taste of his compatriots, and belonging to a genre at the same time solemn, homely, and even frankly popular, peculiar to Austria and south Germany. In them we see the old orchestral suites, cassations, or serenades infinitely rejuvenated and revived by the genius of Mozart, and no study of his symphonic compositions with any pretensions either can or should neglect them.

CHAPTER NINE

Mannheim and Paris (1777–8)

QUARTET (OR 'SINFONIA) CONCERTANTE'
'PARIS' SYMPHONY (K.297)
OVERTURE IN B FLAT

THE GRAND TOUR UNDERTAKEN by Mozart in company with his mother in September 1777, which was to be prolonged until the early part of 1779, marks an epoch of capital importance in his short life. From this time he ceased in some measure to be the Salzburg musician, to become the universal master. It is not the practical result of the journey that should be considered, but rather the considerable enrichment, the broadening, if one may say so, of his art. The young man tasted independence, wider horizons opened before him, grave events ripened him prematurely. The young and agreeable musician of Salzburg was to become, in a few months, the great, the immortal, Mozart.

One feels clearly, moreover, that he had need of a change of air, that the atmosphere of his native town was inadequate, from the sole point of view of instrumental music, to slake his thirst for novelty. So we behold him in Germany's 'symphonic' town *par excellence,* that old Palatinate city wherein instrumental

music had acquired a more weighty importance than
anywhere else. At Mannheim, in fact, each member of
the orchestra seemed to fulfill an official mission, so se-
riously did he take his functions; the wind, notably,
attained a perfection that made an immediate and vivid
impression on Mozart. But—a curious and almost inex-
plicable fact—he did not write a symphony! It is only
much later, in Paris, that he turns to account the essentially 'Mannheimist' resources of the orchestra. In the
meantime he writes only for piano, violin, voice, or
flute, and his music betrays strong French influences.

It is indeed very surprising that a musician such as
Cannabich, whose friend and guest he was, and who
kept him in constant touch with every detail of his own
compositions, never encouraged him to confide to the
admirable orchestra anything more substantial than his
praises. It is true that, if musical interpretation there
was superior, it cannot be said that Mannheim, at the
particular time that Mozart was there, could boast of
anyone to rival Michael Haydn, the Salzburg master, in
musical worth or personal genius. For Mozart the only
person who really counted in this school was old Ignace
Holzbauer, another Viennese, whose *Günther von
Schwarzburg* founded German opera and re-echoed in
the very depths of his soul. This art, strongly tinged
with Italianism, was very much more likely to please
him than that of a Vogler or a Schweitzer, or even—
dare one say it?—a Gluck. And as for the symphonists
past and present of Mannheim, he gives scarcely any
details as to the real value of their works. But he remains
struck in particular by the admirable instrumental ensemble, by the timbres and their effects; especially we
can say that the clarinet was revealed to Mozart during

his stay in Mannheim, and that he was then granted a prophetic glimpse of the marvelous resources it was to offer him in the future.

It is now no longer to be a question of charming Salzburg *divertimenti;* his music henceforward will work toward two main ends: solidity of writing and, especially, a sort of delicately graded precision in the expression of feeling. Until then he had been content to interpret these feelings in general rather than in detail. The new elements absorbed during Mozart's five months at Mannheim are to serve as excellent preparation; he is still in close touch with the prevailing French taste, for the Palatinate was, in fact, a French colony. Karl Theodor, the Elector and reigning sovereign, was a man of entirely French culture; his architects more or less always took their lead from Versailles; all the great 'Mannheim' symphonies of Toëschi and Cannabich, without exception, were sold, published, and played in Paris, so much so that Mozart on arriving in the French capital found himself hearing the Mannheim repertoire all over again at the *Concert Spirituel.* At the outset of his journey he had made contact with 'some quite charming pieces' of the Alsatian Edelmann; then in Paris he renewed acquaintance with Schobert's sonatas and got to know those of Hullmandel. The French influence was therefore at work before his arrival in that country; and before actually arriving in Paris he even wrote some ariettas to French words.

The programs of the great Paris orchestra during the early spring of 1778 were composed mainly of the symphonies of Gossec, whom Mozart had the opportunity of meeting, and of the Abbé Sterkel, whom he reproached for playing too fast; but these programs also

MICHAEL HAYDN Engraving by J. F. Schröter

included Mannheim symphonies, by Toëschi and Cannabich, with in addition numerous *concertantes* designed to group the most diverse virtuosos together and
show off their talents to the best advantage.

   This latter is a genre that we can almost say was born
in Paris, about 1770; public demand was for 'solo' instruments in the symphonies, and the growing taste for
virtuosity especially favored all soloists. Thus, the first
proposition made to Mozart, the day after his arrival in
Paris, concerned Mannheim's four most famous wind
virtuosos, who had come to Paris at the same time as
Mozart. The suggestion was that he should write a
'*symphonie concertante pour la flûte de Wendling, le
hautbois de Ramm, le cor de Punto et le basson de Ritter.*' [1] But, I must add, he changed his mind and substituted for the flute a clarinet, the instrument he was so
captivated by at Mannheim.

   *46—K. Suppl. 9.

   This, which, like the choruses he had written for
Holzbauer's *Miserere*, was prevented from performance by some rather shady intrigues, is a monumental
work, showing no evidence of the haste with which
Mozart confessed he wrote it. It enormously overshadows all the *sinfonie concertante* of the age and even,
by its working out, former ones by Mozart himself, and

----

[1] This work was replaced by a *symphonia concertante* by
Cambini (1746–1823), played by the same quartet (*Concert
Spirituel*, April 12 and 19, 1778).

never again will he give us such an example of the art of
Mannheim. The spacious designs of this great work, one
of the longest he wrote, the marvelous understanding
of the resources of the wind instruments, stamp it as an
altogether unique work, a landmark in the history of
both the symphony and the concerto. It is a direct con-
sequence of his Mannheim visit, and in it we can see the
beginnings of the grand manner of so many of his masterpieces for wind instruments. It is noteworthy that
the three movements of this symphony or quartet *concertante* are all in the same key; their length, with Mozart, indicates importance, according to the popular
taste at Mannheim, and shows him presenting himself
to Paris with a sort of *concerto grosso*, rejuvenated and
brought up to date. There is still no decisive French influence; the work remains German in both conception
and working out. If Mozart wrote it in Paris, it seems
to have been conceived in Mannheim, and at a time
when he had as yet had no direct contact with any
specifically French art; there is in the serenity of the
adagio a kind of religious sentiment akin to Beethoven,
and it is no exaggeration to claim this as one of the greatest moments in all Mozart. The way the ten variations
of the final andantino follow one another, with the intercalated tuttis which never play the theme, but only
the refrain, is itself an inspiration; but the penultimate
one, leading to an adagio recitative that prepares the
way for the final acceleration, once more carries us
toward Beethoven, while the unexpectedness of the
calm before the end removes us from, or rather lifts us
above, the '*thème populaire*' that is the main theme of
this remarkable finale. After all, perhaps the work as a
whole was deemed too different from what the sub-

scribers to the *Concert Spirituel* were accustomed to
hear, and no doubt this is the sole reason why this vast
concerto grosso with which Mozart hoped to make his
Paris debut was never heard.

A compensation for this first failure was not long in
coming. In fact, the performance, in June, of his Symphony in D, called the 'Paris' Symphony (K.297):

*47

concerning which Mozart sent his father some details,
seems to have been a great success. However, in order
probably the more completely to satisfy French tastes,
he entirely remodeled the andante (in G), replacing it
by a new movement, in my opinion more facile and less
banal than the first. This second version has been preserved, and was even published in Sieber's edition.[2]

It must be said at once that at first glance this symphony marks a striking progress from the point of view
of scoring; the Mannheim influence is undeniable. In
this work Mozart, solely to please us, adopts the meth-
ods of the later 'Mannheimists,' in particular those of
his friend Cannabich. This is a question of the precise
attack by the whole orchestra, what was known then
as '*le premier coup d'archet*,' a phrase which has aroused

[2] *Bibliothèque du Conservatoire Paris, Recueil No. 32* (*Symphonies*) '*Du Répertoire du Concert Spirituel: chez le S*r* Sieber,
musicien, rue St-Honoré entre celle des Vielles-Etuves* [sic] *et
celle d'Orléans, chez l'Apothicaire, n*o* 92.*' This was the first
edition.

much sarcasm; of the constant repetition of themes; of the absence of repeat marks; and of an essentially brilliant veneer to the whole work; it seems to me that real French symphonic music had still not reacted on him at the time when he favored us with this 'Paris' Symphony. For who was most frequently performed at the *Concert Spirituel* during his visit? Gossec unquestionably, whom he met, but who seems to have influenced him only during the latter part of his stay in Paris. The symphonies of the Abbé Sterkel were also frequently played, as I have remarked above, also those of Cannabich and Toëschi—without counting the numerous *concertanti* of which the public remained very fond, offering as they did such opportunities to virtuosos of renown.

The conception and composition of the 'Paris' Symphony were clearly influenced by the joy he felt in having at his disposal an admirable body of wind players, in being able worthily to employ each one, drawing from them the effects he so reveled in while at Mannheim. These effects were not used by him until his arrival in Paris, to which the leading players from Mannheim had moved at about the same time. The importance of this orchestra and its resources, which Mozart himself has enumerated,[3] led him to write for a stronger and more compact group than that of Salzburg, moreover a group of players who were often also renowned composers. The symphonic result achieved by Mozart in this, his first composition 'for grand orchestra,' remains, in fact, quite superficial. The admirable unity I have striven so

[3] In a letter to his father, November 4, 1777. '10 or 11 firsts, the same number of seconds, 4 violas, 2 oboes, 2 flutes, 2 clarinets, 2 horns, 4 cellos, 4 bassoons, 4 double basses, trumpets and drums.'

often to emphasize, especially in the symphonies of
1772-3, does not strike us here; there is not that inward
relationship between the different subjects, nor the exquisite originality of invention and working out; they
follow one another without amalgamating, and it must
certainly be conceded that they are somewhat ordinary.
Mozart is so sensitive to every influence that he goes to
the extent of impoverishing his own natural inventive-
ness in order to adopt the imposing but quite empty
framework that distinguishes the greater number of the
Mannheim symphonies; when it was a question of
showing off instrumentalists of the first order he created
a work infinitely greater and more original; his symphony or quartet *concertante* described above seems to
me much more important than the 'Paris' Symphony.
Only the finale of the latter, opening, piano, with the
two violins announcing a *fugato*, greatly heightens the
whole of the symphony; and this anticipation of the
fugato is not wholly deceptive, for the second subject
is ranged in a series of imitations; the repeated antiph-
onal effects between wind and strings certainly make
for variety, and, also, the passage following the second
subject contains a few bars in which we recognize joy-
fully that abrupt change of key so frequent in Mozart's
rapid finales, a sudden veer of the Mozartian fancy
which gives to these few disturbing moments a psychological value perhaps superior to all the rest of the work.
   The best proof that the 'Paris' Symphony decidedly
impressed the patrons of the *Concert Spirituel* is that a
'*Nouvelle symphonie de la composition del Signor
Amadeo Mozart*' figures in the program for September
8, 1778.[4] This had been lost, with the quartet *concer-*

[4] *Journal de Paris*, 1778, p. 987.

tante. Some years ago M. Julien Tiersot discovered in the archives of the Société des Concerts an Overture, in B flat, for grand orchestra, published in parts under the imprint of the Conservatoire.[5] I for my own part have no doubt, after examining the score, that we have here what we are justified in calling Mozart's third French symphonic 'monument.'

It would be difficult, from the purely musical point of view, to detect any correspondence between it and the preceding symphony. Apart from the fact that it is scored for the same orchestra,[6] the language, the style, the inspiration, all are different and, despite the inevitable kinship with Mannheim which, moreover, I have shown to be so agreeable to French taste, we can say with certainty that here Mozart really has appropriated something of contemporary French art. If we were now to seek to enumerate the sources to which he was indebted, we should have before us a large number of comic-opera overtures, Grétry's in particular, which are very likely to have served as models, especially for the andante pastorale that opens the work and serves as an introduction to the allegro con spirito.

The resemblance, however, is only of the most general nature and could quite easily have been evoked by any French Sicilienne. In the symphonic works of Gossec, heard by Mozart at each of the *Concerts Spirituels*, there are some *'points de départ'* infinitely nearer to this B flat Overture. Not that such overtures in one

[5] *Ouverture à grand Orchestre par Mozart.* Prix: 9 fr.—à Paris —à l'Imprimerie du Conservatoire, faubourg Poissonnière, n° 152. Publishers No. 18.

[6] 2 violins (several parts), viola, cello and double bass, 2 flutes, 2 clarinets, 2 horns, 2 oboes, 2 bassoons, 2 trumpets, and drums.

movement, to my knowledge at least, can be found in the purely instrumental work of Gossec (though this would moreover not be impossible), nor that this work can offer examples of counterpoint of such power; but it would hardly be difficult to find in some of the 'pastorales' a similar inspiration. Without venturing outside the French master's opus 5 one can find the very opening of the initial theme of the allegro con spirito of the Overture in B flat.[7]

Was Mozart's aim in writing this work to reduce more and more the extent of a symphony, or to compose a simple overture in the manner of the composers of operas or comic operas? We would be tempted to believe it if we had not long ago established that the first symphonic work he wrote on his return to Salzburg was none other than a similar overture in one movement, packed with French reminiscences, whose dramatic import suggested, wrongly, that we had here the overture to some unknown theatrical piece. The real truth seems to be that Mozart had for nearly a year adopted the framework of the *symphonic overture,* under the direct influence of impressions received in Paris. More, one may add that the clearly symphonic character of the powerful allegro of the B flat Overture has nothing in common with the overture to the ballet *Les Petits Riens*—very light and barely tinged with '*turquerie*'— which does approach more nearly those of the masters of French comic opera.[8]

The extreme diversity of Mozart's Parisian impressions is apparent in technical procedures that, one feels

[7] *Symphonie,* op. 5, no. 1.
[8] See Hermann Abert: *W. A. Mozart,* Vol. I, pp. 733 ff.

certain, he would never have used if his memorable sojourn in Paris had not taken place. Alike in his piano,
chamber, and orchestral music there are such novelties,
a spirit so removed from that of Salzburg, something so
pompous, such a feeling of effort, so studied and not
without a certain sense of strain, that one is almost dis-
concerted. And such are the feelings one experiences in
the presence of this astonishing Overture in B flat. We
have here a veritable upheaval in the work and convic-
tions of the young Mozart; the piano sonatas in A minor,
those for piano and violin in E minor, the *sinfonia concertante* for the Mannheim soloists—all these, one after
another, preceding this overture, give place to a quite
chaotic phase in the rapid flowing of the Mozartian
flood. It can be said of most of these works, as of the
present overture, that we have here a great mind ex-
posed to all manner of external attractions; each of these
works taken by itself shows us, often with considerable
force, a Mozart in the act of discovering some entirely
new idea, models for which, it is gratifying to note, can
be found in French music; taken as a whole, it is difficult
to believe that these works belong to the same creative
period. And moreover, in studying attentively a work
such as this B flat Overture, we cannot, despite its power
and real beauty, help being struck by something working rather in a void, something which, as in several
works of this period, at times gives, too, the impression
of skimpiness. All this, moreover, will need nearly another year for it to be thoroughly assimilated; only in
the works dating from 1779–80 shall we see the full frui-
tion of Mozart's grand tour.

   On the whole, his symphonic production during his
stay in Paris shows him evolving by clearly marked

stages toward the French style; [9] still very Mannheimist in the quartet *concertante*, he conforms more to
French taste in the 'Paris' Symphony, though still remaining faithful to the Mannheim school; the Overture
in B flat shows him already a slave to French manners
and customs, but with a persistent dramatic idea such as
is apparent in the symphonies and overtures of a Gossec
or a Gluck.

I feel I ought to give here a few brief details of
this Overture in B flat, which is not available in a modern edition; the themes are worthy of notice, if only to
give an idea of the quality of Mozart's inspiration during the latter part of his stay in Paris.

The overture opens, as I have said, with an andante
pastorale (K. Suppl. 8):

*48

34 bars long, the theme allotted to the first oboe solo,
accompanied by sustained chords on the strings. I need
not here stress its typically French character, reminding
us at once of Grétry. The first violin replies to this in a
passage linking it to the allegro spiritoso:

*49

[9] Parisian symphonies '*del signor Amedeo Mozart*' continue
to figure in the programs of the *Concert Spirituel:* March 18,
March 28, May 23, June 3, 1779 (advertisements in the *Journal de
Paris*).

I have already compared this with a symphony by Gossec (op. 5, no. 1), of which the following are the opening measures:

*50

This first subject, repeated, leads to a theme of martial character:

*51

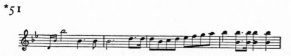

briefly rounded off by a concluding ritornello in the dominant. Then begins a true development on the first subject, which is repeated at the commencement in the original key. A new cadence in the dominant ensues, and a solo for the bassoons:

*52

The bassoons are soon joined by the flute alone, and then comes a little *fugato* leading to the recapitulation. This begins strictly, but is modified after the following fashion: the ritornello of the first part is suppressed; instead, a development of a passage that has figured in the ritornello here serves to separate the two expositions of this first subject. This second appearance of the first subject corresponds fairly closely with the second exposition in the first part; but this time a passage is momentarily suppressed to make room for a return of the beautiful bassoon theme, this time played by flute and oboe in the tonic. After that, a ritornello on the first violin (in triplets) leads to the suppressed passage, adorned with a brilliant final ritornello. The scoring is distinguished by contrapuntal force, solidity, and marvelous brilliance.

CHAPTER TEN

The Return to Germany (1779–80)

SYMPHONY IN G (K.318)
SYMPHONY IN B FLAT (K.319)
SERENADE IN D (K.320)
CONCERTANTE FOR VIOLIN AND VIOLA (K.364)
SYMPHONY IN C (K.338)

SINCE MOZART DURING THE years 1775 to 1777, both
before his great Mannheim tour and while he was in
France, wrote no symphonies properly so called, one
may well feel some astonishment on finding him, once
more returned to Salzburg, applying rapidly the tech-
niques that have just revealed to him a school very different from that of his native town. Whether this unexpected recrudescence of his symphonic productivity
was the result of an order from the Archbishop, or
whether it was simply one more indication of his interest in orchestration, we cannot say; but we may well believe that, back in this narrow and backward town that
he disliked, he could not resist the temptation to give his
compatriots some idea of both Parisian tastes and his
own improved abilities. From all the memories seething
in his brain he chooses first of all something heroic, pathetic, something at the same time very frank and clean

in expression, with new and very varied nuances. This something was the outcome of a very real intercourse with the French masters and, although he remains absolutely silent on the subject, probably also with the opera or the comic opera. All the projects he had cherished in this regard in France came to nothing, and these frustrations must undoubtedly have helped to embitter him and indispose him toward the French: Mozart owed us, in fact, a lyric tragedy, *Alexandre et Roxane*, both poet and libretto of which remained unknown to him. But we can console ourselves with the fact that these preparatory studies of Mozart and his father's counsel on the subject of French taste led up to Wolfgang's first dramatic masterpiece, the lyric tragedy *Idomeneo*, whose origins can be traced back to that same Lemierre,[1] the author of *La Veuve de Malabar*, previously mentioned.

There is already a touch of *Idomeneo* in the first symphony, in G (K.318), written by Mozart two months after returning to Salzburg:

*53

the theatrical flavor might even suggest an overture, though otherwise there is no justification for such an opinion. The work, a curious one, full of innovations, written in a single movement (there is a slow movement in the middle, followed by an abridged reprise of the

[1] Antoine-Marin Lemierre (1720–93).

first part, as a coda), shows to what extent Mozart had remained impressed by the *opera seria* overtures he had heard in Paris; its explanation is much simpler now that the B flat Overture is known to us. On the eve of quitting Paris, Mozart, probably influenced by Gossec or other masters of French opera, writes a symphonic overture in one movement; the moment he finds himself back in the calm of Salzburg we have another work of precisely similar character, just as compact and dramatic, and equally with no precise object in view. Note too that the scoring of the two works is the same, except for the clarinets, missing at Salzburg; but the Parisian work is the stronger contrapuntally, and the whole is in general much more elaborate and developed; the Symphony in G, though barer, is not less strong, and unexpected modulations are not lacking; what is more, the middle andante has a character so Mozartian that we feel ourselves on the brink of his maturity. The Symphony in G is one of the most convincing proofs of the profound change that has come about in Mozart during his long tour; there is nothing in it of the old Salzburg style, and if he had continued to write in this style one would have been almost justified in saying that Gluck or Gossec had definitely replaced Michael or Josef Haydn in his heart! The particular spirit and style of this symphony are going to make way for other tendencies, until the moment when the Abbé Varesco, adapting the French work of the curious Lemierre to the taste of Salzburg or Munich, evokes the same inspiration, the same brass writing, sometimes the same dissonances. It is needless to add that in all this we have the technique of the Mannheim school used with increasing purpose: powerful crescendos, a freer interchange of musical ideas between *soli* and *tutti,* masterly use of the wind, and so on.

Some months later, at the beginning of July 1779, Mozart in the Symphony in B flat (K.319):

*54

draws for us a delightful picture of a beautiful summer's day; we could almost describe it as his 'pastoral' symphony. It is full of gusto, joy, dancing, not unmixed with a certain sensual ecstasy (in the first movement), expressed by numerous and insistent chromaticisms. This first allegro (3/4) has the captivating undulation of a Viennese waltz; it has no repeat bars, nor could it have, since from the opening to the final coda the dance movement persists without pause. The symphony originally had but three movements; the minuet was added later, in Vienna, accentuating still more the general character of the work. There is, it has even been suggested,[2] a certain resemblance to Schubert, whose name springs involuntarily to mind. But where has Mozart had the opportunity of breathing these rare Viennese perfumes? We seem to hear popular tunes of the Austrian capital in the finale—a joyous melee, after the lyrical repose offered us in the andante, very skillfully conceived in the taste of the times. Here is certainly a work imbued with the Viennese spirit, abounding in delicious rhythmic and harmonic details, which, indeed, have no

[2] Abert, op. cit., Vol. I, p. 806, note 2.

point in common with the highly dramatic quality of
the preceding Symphony in G. In the latter there is no
difficulty in recognizing the dramatic influence, as it
were a premonition of *Idomeneo*, but I think it would
be much more troublesome to discover in contemporary Viennese masters, the Vanhalls and Dittersdorfs,
any work analogous to this B flat Symphony. It is,
taken as a whole, a mirror of the pure genius of Mozart.

This Viennese spirit, compounded of delicate playfulness and artless sensuality, continues to be evident in a
series of works by Mozart, and is to find an interpreter
of similar caliber in certain works by the young Schubert; it is, too, a spirit pervading many a cassation or
serenade, of which Mozart typifies the highest expression. Since accomplishing his grand tour, however, some
foreign elements have intruded, and it is found only
rarely in its former purity; we must wait until the last
year of Mozart's life, when, transfigured, purified by
celestial appeasement, it will attain its uttermost beauty.

We do not know the motive behind the appearance
of a grand Serenade (K.320):

*55

still in the customary key of D, dated August 1779: it is
as it were the pendant to the Haffner music of 1776, but
enriched by all that Mozart had gained since that time.
Seeing the introductory prelude suddenly reappearing
toward the middle of the first movement, we cannot but

Title page of the first edition of the Symphony in B flat major (K. 319)

recall the experiment in the preceding Symphony in G, of interrupting a grand allegro by a slow movement; but here the originality is greater since the function of an introduction is normally confined to the first measures of a movement. The irresistible urge of the first subject of the allegro allows no time for the other subjects to expand and develop; its flood sweeps all before it. Everything in this serenade seems to violate custom or to break a rule; the profound, almost tragic character of grief with no hope of consolation gives the andante (in D minor) an atmosphere corresponding to nothing in the usual andantes of the serenades. One might ask here if Mozart is not bidding farewell to some friendship, some deep emotion of long standing; and this suggestion seems confirmed by the 'posthorn' calls in the trio of the following minuet.[3]

The concerto which it was customary to intercalate in these serenades is here a *Sinfonia concertante* (for two flutes, two oboes, two bassoons), clearly a souvenir of the work written on his arrival in Paris, but in which we meet once again the cordial and intimate Salzburg spirit. It must not be forgotten that we are now in fact in the prime of the *sinfonia concertante*, and that we must wait until Mozart arrives in Vienna before he writes a true concerto for a solo instrument. Until then his practice will be to group together diverse 'solo' instruments, as he did in Paris and Mannheim; and these groupings, as far as the orchestral part is concerned, give rise to real symphonic works that could not be omitted in a historical review of Mozart's symphonies.[4]

[3] Abert, op. cit., Vol. I, p. 811.
[4] The great piano concertos of his maturity would themselves deserve study from a purely symphonic point of view.

So we find that the *Sinfonia concertante* for violin and viola:

*56—K.364:

written toward the end of 1779, is comparable in proportions to the Quartet *concertante* of Paris, and just as Mannheimist in treatment. Mozart here definitely returns to a taste long appreciated in his own country; he gives us a sort of dialogue, or grand duo, between two instruments that are almost the personification of the two performers. The orchestra is really imposing, with its long train of trills in the cellos, beneath tremolando strings, and its fixed tonality (E flat); it is persistently Mannheimist, and one could readily believe it intended for some of the Mannheim virtuosos, Fränzl or Eck for example, rather than the ordinary run of players at Salzburg. Moreover, we do not know the occasion that called forth this great work. It is noble and passionate, and it is not difficult to see in it an anticipation of several of the works of the master's maturity in the same key, E flat, which are analogous in feeling with this work—for different keys represented for Mozart particular modes of poetic expression. The plaintive and somber andante is a sort of elegy, the sordins, as it were, stifling the sobs; it is one of those painful, even poignant moments that are far from rare in Mozart. The inspiration is akin to that of the preceding andante—that of the great serenade composed in August—though much

sadder. Thus everything leads us to believe that the
concertante dates from the following autumn. As for the
finale, it is a quick movement well calculated to dispel
the shades so lately all around us.[5]

One might almost call the present the symphonic
period of Mozart's life: the period of the *sinfonia concertante*. In fact, the effect of all that he had learned at
Mannheim or Paris was chiefly a stressing of some one
instrument, or category of instruments, in the ensemble.
And then the opportunity to write for a whole series of
eminent soloists tended to emphasize the *concertante*
spirit, which shows itself in a variety of manners, in a
variety of instrumental groupings. Later all will be used;
the musical ensemble will absorb technical innovations,
and once more the development of instrumental virtuosity will be found to have made a notable contribution,
to have enriched and enlarged the whole field of music.

The present period closes with a work that has points
of resemblance to that which opened it; that is to say,
the Symphony in G. The resemblance is particularly in
the heroic character of its first movement: it is a Symphony in C major:

*57—K.338.

[5] This period, the heyday of the *sinfonia concertante*, gave us
another work of Mozart, unfinished; it is the opening portion,
fairly extensive, of a similar Symphony for violin, viola, and cello
in A (K. Supplement 104). It is scored for the same orchestra as
the *concertante* for violin and viola.

with all the qualities associated with this key. Finished on August 29, 1780, one can already imagine Mozart thinking in the heroic accents of *Idomeneo;* the symphony opens with an imposing vigor in the clear and almost bare tonality of C major, but almost immediately there are romantic nuances to color and vary the picture. There are sudden alternations of major and minor, a multitude of themes, and a romantic development of a novel character, which, in spite of that, is linked to the first part in unaccountable fashion. The concluding pianissimo produces something of the same effect as the end of the development of the great E flat Symphony (1788); as in the preceding symphonies this first movement has no repeats, but is built rather in the manner of an overture; it ends with an almost triumphal coda on the proud and martial first subject. The whole is primarily heroic and brilliant; but how strongly one feels that Mozart was scarcely ever capable of writing a movement simply and solely heroic and brilliant! This movement is strewn with contrasts resulting from abrupt modulations; and then the unexpected nature of the development gives quite a modern impression, fleetingly almost Schumannesque. It is hard to understand how this work has until quite lately impressed solely by its superficial character, and how the novelty and variety of its nuances remain still unperceived.

It is particularly difficult for me to express my thoughts concerning the andante di molto, scored for strings with the addition of a solitary flute. There are short moments in life which defy explanation, it may be because their unexpected variety remains untranslatable, or rather because their brevity and charm have a unique character—that is to say, never reappear. It is a

question of something indefinite, but of which one feels
any return or revival is impossible. Well, it is such a
moment as this, in its apparent simplicity, that reveals
this andante to us, with a delicacy and emotion we have
never paralleled even in the work of Mozart.

The Symphony in C included a minuet, which was
never completed and which Mozart suppressed.[6] As for
the finale, it has an energy and fire that set it apart in the
master's symphonic work; it suggests a sort of tarantella
carrying all before it in its passionate *élan*. The themes
are diversified, but never interrupt this lively rhythm;
on the contrary, each seems to supplement the other, to
give still more force to the whole movement. In one of
his letters Mozart tells us he had to direct this symphony: 'It went *magnifique*. There were forty violins.' [7]
We see from this that Mozart was not dismayed by an
orchestral mass, and that his symphonies were designed
for large combinations of instruments. This one marks,
from the symphonic standpoint, the onset of his full
mastery, to be more and more rapidly accentuated during the few years of his glorious and brief maturity.

If we now inquire what were Mozart's varied tendencies during this period, we must recognize that the
French influence is in general the dominant one, despite
the Viennese style and the survival of the Italian form.

[6] The original manuscript of the symphony belongs today to
the Library of the Paris Conservatoire, from the Malherbe be-
quest.

[7] Mozart's Letters, April 11, 1781. See *Letters of Mozart and
His Family*, translated by Emily Anderson, Vol. III, p. 1076. Mo-
zart adds: 'the wind instruments were all doubled, there were ten
violas, ten double basses, eight violoncellos, and six bassoons.'
(But see also Tovey: *Essays in Musical Analysis*, Vol. I, p. 181.)
(Tr.)

Sometimes, too, the master seems to draw near to
Haydn, but at the same time decidedly following his
own bent, and we feel from now on that Mozart's genius
is already so sure of itself, so powerful, that he can be
content to borrow a procedure or a form from one or
the other, but that his language and technique are now
definitely formed, that the unshakable foundations of
this language are already laid.

This period of mellowing and deepening, spent entirely in the calm of Salzburg, gave him the opportunity
to absorb and fuse forever in one crucible all the new
instrumental devices, all the impressions gained in Mannheim and Paris. He is to turn them to account and give
us the true meaning and right application in the tragedy
Idomeneo, already in his head; this is the goal to which
all the striving, all the experiments—in a nutshell, all the
riches and inventions gained from the most memorable
of all his travels—are leading.

CHAPTER ELEVEN

Vienna (1781–6)

SYMPHONY-SERENADE IN D (K.385), 1782
SYMPHONY IN C, THE 'LINZ'(K.425), 1783
FUNERAL ODE (K.477), 1785

M ORE THAN A YEAR after he finally settled in Vienna,[1]
Mozart made the acquaintance of a rich amateur,
Baron van Swieten, through whom he gradually came to
know and understand the principal masterpieces of the
old masters. Van Swieten not only implanted an admiration for Bach and Handel that was to last to the end of
his days, but charged him with the thankless task of
'reorchestrating' several of the latter's most celebrated
works. Mozart was also expected to take part in performances at the house of his new patron; he had to direct many a choral or instrumental work of Handel or
Bach, and no more was needed to make him an immediate convert to these two great men. The moment had
arrived when counterpoint and fugue were to give rise
to numerous attempts at elaboration and rejuvenation;
and while their beauty and grandeur are revived in him,
counterpoint and fugue become his favorite modes of

---

[1] Mozart arrived in Vienna on March 16, 1781, having been
summoned there from Salzburg by the Archbishop. (Tr.)

expression. His contrapuntal haste and fever is so great that a number of works remain unfinished, and looking over them one cannot help bitterly regretting this incomplete state. Moreover, another revelation, equally important artistically, led to a fresh conception of rondo form and incited him to throw off some admirable fantasias, which show him freely improvising at the piano; a result, this, of reading Emanuel Bach, which we can also attribute to the new intimacy with van Swieten. One can see how during this period of his life he was leaving Viennese taste behind him, and can realize the value for him of this enthusiastic study of great classical music.

In the symphonic field this double, illustrious, and salutary influence revealed itself on the eve of the production of *Die Entführung aus dem Serail* in a totally unexpected manner. Mozart, overburdened with work, receives an urgent command from Salzburg: it is the end of July 1782, and the Haffner family are imploring another symphony to add to the brilliance of the family gathering.[2] Mozart hastily sets to work (July 20, 1782).

But what changes! What will his fellow townsmen say to this? The opening of his new Symphony-Serenade (K.385):

*58

Allegro con spirito

[2] The occasion was the ennobling of Siegmund Haffner, Elisabeth Haffner's brother. (Tr.)

with no prelude (save the indispensable march [8]) presents us with a long and severe, even aggressive theme,
which is going to occupy the whole movement, with
only a few interruptions by rapid ritornelli. There is no
second subject. The movement is a *fugato* in which
harsh and incisive seconds succeed each other with but
little respite. We are several hundred leagues from the
brilliant and flowing movements we are accustomed to
hear in the shades of Salzburg. But the master had forgotten these times. He could not bring himself straight
from the pages of Bach or Handel back to the old
charming and facile manner so much in vogue in his
native town. So he presents the respectable burghers of
his own land with one of the most audacious works ever
entrusted by him to an orchestra: audacious, first, in its
archaic style highly spiced with the harmonic tang with
which Mozart so often offends the somewhat amor-
phous palate of his contemporaries; second, by the
unique subject that provides the substance of the piece.
This is, indeed, something quite exceptional, something
Mozart himself has never dared risk in a true symphony.
And see too what infinite variety is imposed on this
theme by modulations of a boldness unsurpassed or
even unapproached by anyone of his epoch. Those of
the development, in particular, are so hazardous that it
is surprising that they have passed without protest from
ignoramuses or pedants; these might well have given
rise to the very ungracious sort of criticism that has been
provoked by the first bars of the last of the six quartets
dedicated to Josef Haydn.

The first movement is in sonata form, despite its

[8] K.408, No. 2. (Tr.)

contrapuntal character; though it is deprived of repeat
marks, one can see quite clearly where they would be:
namely, after a symphonic ritornello such as can be
found elsewhere in other symphonies of Mozart, leading to the dominant. So here we behold an important
work, to open one of the richest periods in Mozart's life;
everything in this life presents a sort of harmony, and
one cannot forbear to observe that if the Vienna period
opens, in the symphonic field, with this unexpected
homage to the language of the old masters, it will likewise end with a composition which is, as it were, the
apotheosis of counterpoint and fugue, the final goal of
all his instrumental career revivified by a return to all
that is greatest and most solid in the past, and what has
already been called Mozart's symphonic testament: the
finale of his last, the 'Jupiter' Symphony.

The rest of this "Haffner" music, particularly the
andante and the minuet—there had originally been a
second, suppressed when this symphony-serenade was
performed in 1783 at one of his Viennese concerts—is
much more in keeping with the original purpose of the
music and needs no special comment; but the finale has
a verve and animation which it is no exaggeration to say
approaches that of the *Figaro* overture. We sense here,
from the very beginning, a clear reminder of the recent
Entführung aus dem Serail, a sketch of the terror and
buffoonery of Osmin; the life, spirit, and energy of this
finale make it a work of a delicacy and fervor without
precedent. Toward the end a sort of coda adds to the
unexpectedness; it is impossible at this point of exultation and ecstasy not to be reminded of Josef Haydn and
his habit of redoubling the gaiety of his finales toward
the end.

It is clear that at this particular moment of his sojourn in Vienna Mozart had no other model so far as the orchestra was concerned, and it must be stated once more that Haydn was then reigning in Vienna with almost unrivaled glory. Moreover, 1782 was the year in which the younger master set to work composing the first of the six quartets, to be offered three years later to his illustrious confrere and elder; so his ears would certainly, and very naturally, be full of Haydn's latest compositions. And the relations between the two great men had become, or were about to become, much more cordial; Leopold Mozart's visit to his son in 1785, and the dedication of the six quartets to Josef Haydn, helped to reinforce the existing bonds, and to make Haydn's influence much more noticeable; while for the same reason Mozart's influence on Haydn continued to grow.

It is the general opinion that in the C major Symphony (K.425):

*59

composed at Linz and dated November 3, 1783, the acme of Haydn's influence is reached. The character of the introductory adagio, the theme and the march rhythms of the succeeding allegro spiritoso, the development section of the final presto, and so forth, are instanced as direct reflections of the art of the Esterház master. It is certain that this symphony, which truly opens the period of Mozart's great orchestral compositions, is akin to Haydn's symphonies in certain obvious

ways, if one wished to find an absolute model for it—
notably in the prevailing mood of the finale, and also in
the working-out of the development of this entrancing
movement. All this is indisputable. But, to my mind,
Mozart's individuality is so overwhelmingly apparent
in the symphony as a whole that it is scarcely possible, at
this stage of his growth, to imagine any inspiration
from without; to Mozart, and to Mozart alone, belong
the varied shades of feeling in the first movement—
nuances often attributable to the well-managed use of
contrast between wind and strings; his, too, is the march
that runs through this movement, at once warlike and
dreamy. And to what, if not the profound genius of
Mozart, do we owe the wonderful and touching beauty
of the poco adagio? The somber clouds that momentarily tarnish its pure and serene inspiration neither
form nor dissolve in the manner of Haydn; in its complexity it is already the grand adagio of the classical
symphony in which one feels that the last word has been
said. It is certainly not easy to understand how Mozart,
taken unprepared by old Count Thun on his arrival at
Linz, could in the space of a few short days have accomplished such a feat; it seems likely that the conception of
the symphony was an accomplished fact before he left
Salzburg, where he had just spent a holiday, and that he
had to do no more than write it down some time between his departure and his return.

The minuet is one of the most celebrated; one is liable
to find it anywhere. We have seen it figuring in what is
called the 'ballet' in *Don Giovanni,* and in the short
dances in *Figaro.* The fact is, it is more suitable for
dancing than symphonic minuets in general are; and
even in the trio, also in C major, its charming, soft light

is maintained; the way the theme of this trio is taken up
in imitation is unrivaled in any similar passage of Mozart. As for the finale, I willingly concede that the
shadow of the great Haydn is discernible, but I must add
at once that the variety of emotions and the undercur-
rent of passionate uneasiness give it so Mozartian a quality as soon as the composer gets into his subject that the
very intention of following a model is effaced, and all
previous suggestions become subject to an inner world
of his own. It cannot be denied, however, that the treatment of the development section and the rapid passages
preceding the ends of both parts derive from Haydn;
these passages apart, the whole symphony stands as a
pure and noble creation of Mozart, now in the full
bloom of his maturity.

If, moreover, the chronological list of Haydn's symphonies is examined with any care, one cannot but be
struck by the very small number of those dated between
1780 and 1782 whose introduction gives rise to a slow
movement, and in general the symphonies of the Esterház master scarcely show any clear points of comparison
with the "Linz" Symphony before those that he wrote
for Paris and London.[4] In comparing the "Linz" Symphony with Haydn's works, no one has envisaged the
much more probable case of the reaction of this symphony on the elder composer's art. And, frankly, who
knows to what ideals the young master was wedded in
the autumn of this year 1783? When he returned to
Vienna and had to write this Symphony in C major on
his Linz visit, he most certainly had with him a symphony by his old master and Salzburg friend, Michael

[4] See the catalogue that heads the great Breitkopf edition of
Haydn's symphonies.

Haydn, who, delighted to meet his erstwhile pupil again, gave him, as a souvenir of past times, one of his latest symphonies, written in the spring of the same year. Until recent times this symphony was attributed to Mozart, who had taken the trouble to copy out the parts himself with a view to its performance at one of his Vienna concerts, or perhaps even at Linz to meet the immediate needs of a concert organized by Count Thun, the dedicatee of the Symphony in C we are dealing with. At this period in his artistic career Mozart seems to have regarded a slow introduction as almost indispensable for the opening of a grand symphony; and in fact he wrote an adagio to serve as an introduction to this symphony of Michael Haydn. The result is that people have believed themselves faced with an authentic Mozart symphony. The symphony in question is that in G, bearing the number 444 of Köchel's catalogue: [5]

*60

It is difficult to comprehend how the editors of the great Breitkopf edition of Mozart could have considered the three movements of the G major Symphony as the immediate successors of the 'Linz' Symphony; the infinitely simpler and more archaic art of the Salzburg master offers such a contrast that one might well suppose this symphony to date much earlier than 1783, actually the year of its birth. But the important point to

[5] K. (3rd ed.) 425a. (Tr.)

COUNT FRANZ ESTERHÁZY OF GALÁNTA   Mezzotint after a painting
by F. Palko by J. G. Haid, Vienna, 1769

note is this choice of Mozart, for whom the instrumental
work of his old master had retained its value and importance. It proves in what high esteem Mozart held him;
and up to the present no one has discovered any composition by Josef Haydn that he has taken the trouble
not only to copy out in his own hand but in addition to
adorn with an expressive prelude, which, moreover, is
by no means entirely in key with the movement it is
intended to prepare.

Two years elapsed before an unexpected event occurred, offering Mozart the opportunity of writing, not
a new symphony, but a short funeral ode to the memory
of two brother Freemasons: Duke George Augustus of
Mecklenburg-Strelitz and Count Franz Esterházy of
Galánta, Chancellor of Hungary and Grand Master of
the lodge to which Mozart belonged (November 1785)
(K.477):

*61

This is a short movement of the utmost significance. The
composition of the orchestra is itself peculiar; besides
the string quartet it includes two oboes, one clarinet,
two horns, three basset horns, and a double bassoon.
Around a *cantus firmus* of liturgical origin the orchestra
weaves arabesques with a most modern effect; harmonies to be met again only in the first pages of the
Requiem rend the noble meditation of the opening;

then comes a march rhythm depicting almost visibly the double funeral, accompanying the *cantus firmus.* When the *cortège* arrives, there breaks out a note of agony, which, in due course, is expressed only in short sobs, more and more widely spaced, leading to a dull resignation quenched at last in a final major chord, pianissimo. This spirit of profound resignation, free from all revolt, and likewise far removed from any weakness in the face of death, reveals the very depths of Mozart's confident and Christian soul.

This funeral ode, despite its brevity, is a symphony. It remains almost completely unknown; nevertheless, as much by its instrumental treatment as by its psychological insight, it is one of the most important moments Mozart ever experienced. And it provides the occasion to repeat that the use of wind instruments here reaches heights that are still unsuspected. Mozart, as far back as 1785, using similar resources, has here written an instrumental prelude to his Requiem.

CHAPTER TWELVE

The 'Prague' Symphony
(December 6, 1786)

*62—K.504.

SOME MONTHS AFTER *Le Nozze di Figaro* Mozart en-
tered on a period of artistic growth that was to yield
fruits so numerous and so rich that it is astonishing to
see the majority of biographies so little impressed with
the fact. Both the expression and the form of his work
will grow and intensify; they will give to his work a
range infinitely greater and higher, with more force and
bolder relief; and one can say that this period, closing
with *Don Giovanni* and the great symphonies, marks
the most truly 'romantic' epoch of his career. For freedom, originality, and poetry it compares with that of his
last visit to Italy, in 1773, with the addition, naturally,
of the ripening of a genius that has attained, or is shortly
to attain, its fullest radiance. But to reach the middle of
this period Mozart must go through some months of
transition when, perhaps under the influence of a man

too unjustly disdained by him, Muzio Clementi, he will be striving to elaborate long movements built on a single subject, uniting consummate science with the divine fire of his genius. It is particularly noteworthy that, in this transitory period, it is principally the works for piano that benefit by this newly acquired power, which makes it all the more probable that the Italian master's influence was then acting on him with peculiar force. The piano sonatas, trios, and concertos particularly show this sort of progress, visible, one might say, at the very first glance.

It was at the end of these few months that he had to write, for an occasion that has remained unknown, the Symphony in D (K.504) known as the "Prague" Symphony.[1] It would seem that everything Mozart intended for the inhabitants and connoisseurs of that city was invested with a quite peculiar fire and animation; he felt almost certain of being thoroughly and profoundly understood there. And this is no small encouragement to the artist, nor is it less a merit in those who bring it about. We know, too, in what enthusiastic terms he spoke of his Prague friends after *Don Giovanni.*

His first knock on their door was with the Symphony in D, re-echoing with a rough, a solid assurance. The success was equal to its anticipation. In listening to this symphony one has sometimes—nay, often—the impression of being in the presence of Beethoven, so closely are the grandeur of design and the vigor with which it is realized bound together; that enormous prelude with its intensifying rising phrases, and the modulations of the

[1] The first edition of this symphony, by André of Offenbach (op. 87), was advertised in July 1801 (*Allgemeine Musikalische-Zeitung*).

little '*gruppetti*' motif, herald events so solemn that one
is almost astonished on hearing the principal theme of
the allegro, passionately 'modern' in character, its feverish syncopations contrasting with the heroic interruptions from the brass. One has a striking impression of
novelty, as much in the inspiration as in the scoring and
harmony of all this movement. Mozart here no longer
speaks the language we have met in his former compositions; we get the impression that this language is entirely
his own creation, and we know of no musician who
might have been able to reveal its elements to him. Perhaps if we were forced to choose one the name of
Clementi would again present itself most readily to our
mind. We have a foreshadowing of *Die Zauberflöte*, not
only in the cast of the ideas themselves but in the effects
obtained by means of counterpoint; and this symphony
would be memorable if only from this point of view.
The whole of the development is significant in this respect and, I would say, unique as a precursor of things
to come; and the way in which the recapitulation is
modulated and varied is also absolutely characteristic in
its astonishing modernism. The romantic criticism of
Mozart that sees in him nothing but an Olympic god,
eternally serene, never experiencing the troubles or
anxieties of mortal uneasiness, seems to me quite incom-
prehensible, the more so since this D major Symphony
is by no means an isolated phenomenon in his work.

Another matter for surprise awaits us in this first
movement, which we might readily expect to see built
entirely on the first subject, followed by rhythmic figures on the brass and vigorous contrapuntal designs; it
is the presence, nevertheless, of a second subject, but
relegated to the very end of the first part and then

quickly hurried through. Mozart, after some months
during which, probably under Clementi's influence, he
schooled himself to build his first allegros on a single
subject, returned gradually to the contrast of two subjects; and thus the D major Symphony clearly marks the
end of the transition period I mentioned above.

It would be difficult to employ chromaticisms and
counterpoint with a more constant subtlety than in the
andante (in G major), in which feelings of such variety
are so intermingled that a new and enchanted world
seems to open before our eyes for the first time. I feel
myself quite powerless to describe it; we recognize in
this marvelous and most musical reverie something pastoral or idyllic; but for all the singing of birds and the
murmuring of waters, fleeting clouds often come to
darken the landscape. There are sometimes even cries of
anguish to be heard; but nature's all-pervading peace
soon regains the mastery, and, despite most intense and
modern dissonances, despite modulations that vary the
first subject at each repetition during the development,
the movement ends on a note of inward peace, of poetic
repose. Perhaps it is permissible to find here something
akin to the feeling, not easily definable, that emerges
from the 'scene by the brook,' a feeling that only the
very greatest poets have been able to suggest; and it is
certainly not the much vaunted simplicity of Mozart
that reigns here! This movement proves the richness and
variety of his inner life; it also proves him to have been
intensely moved by the most intimate and subtle poetry
of nature.

The finale, whose initial rhythm recalls the short duet
in *Figaro* where Cherubino escapes by jumping through
a window, is, like the other two movements, built with

the rigorous symmetry of sonata form. To my mind, whatever one may say, it is again one wherein joy is not unalloyed; a burning, ardent passion creeps in and, despite its opening, it is rather of the ardors of the almost contemporary *Don Giovanni* that this finale reminds us. There are, moreover, certain aspects in which this symphony is akin to the famous overture to *Don Giovanni*. Elements of drama and joy are, in fact, closely intermingled; the symphony certainly ends on the latter note, but on some abrupt, almost lacerating rhythms that suggest more of struggle and energy than of real happiness. We do not know what hindered Mozart from writing a minuet for this symphony; perhaps the total exclusion of dancing is deliberate or, in any case, more usual in Prague than in Vienna.

CHAPTER THIRTEEN

A Musical Joke, or A Symphonic Caricature (June 14, 1787)

*63—K.522.

THIS WORK, OFTEN DESIGNATED 'The Village Musicians' or 'Peasant Symphony,' is actually entitled 'A Musical Joke' (*Ein musikalischer Spass*). It is thus headed by Mozart himself in the catalogue of his works.

Everyone seems to have been totally mistaken as to the real idea behind this parody, and Hermann Abert, the greatest modern biographer of Mozart, opens up new avenues in this connection in the second volume of his remarkable work.[1] What has until now been taken for a satire on the playing of poor and unskilled musicians is really directed much more against the infatuated ignorance of the composer aspiring to write something resembling—however faintly—a symphony. It is not the deliberately falsified cadences or passages which

[1] Hermann Abert: *W. A. Mozart*, Vol. II, pp. 394 ff.

'misfire' that ought to attract our attention so much as the grotesque emptiness and the only too obvious incompetence of the so-called composer. Most assuredly Mozart must have had some 'model' in writing this curious work, and we can certainly speak of influence here though we do not know the person aimed at.

He adopts the older symphonic framework, using strings and two horns; or rather he was thinking of the *divertimento,* then very much the fashion in Vienna since it gave many a composer the chance of a quick popularity. These works were heard in the salons, also in the open air in fine weather, so that opportunity for them to become known was not lacking.

The most striking thing about this parody of a symphony is the fundamental incapacity of the composer to bind two ideas together in any logical sequence whatever; this incapacity is such that, in the first movement particularly (for the *Spass* includes four movements in the style of a true symphony), there are whole passages with merely an accompaniment droning away in the basses and violas, with no additional part to give sense to this meaningless murmur; and then, even the most elementary sense of modulation invariably fails the composer every time he needs it. Clearly Mozart had not the intention of presenting the insufferable spectacle of a tyro attempting to handle the full orchestra; he has chosen, with impeccable taste, the more modest canvas of the *divertimento* or sextet with two horns; at the same time the idea is to produce something resembling or even giving the illusion of a symphony such as was still in vogue during Mozart's youth.

The long and ungainly *fioriture* in the slow movement seem to suggest an overambitious violinist, but also

reveal to us a composer who is prey to the worst senti-
mentality, endeavoring to interpret it by scrappy bits of
tune and excessive digressions. The *longueurs* of this
movement are perhaps even surpassed by the trio of the
minuet, cut to a most unusual pattern; some timid attempts at counterpoint usher in the repeat of the minuet.
But the finale is, perhaps, the most remarkable of all; the
composer here risks an actual *fugato*, which stops short
after four measures, as in fact do most of his ideas. It is a
hotchpotch of unrelated themes, with no logical order
to it; one senses a mind more fertile in the attempt than
in the realization. But we have here a veritable rondo,
full of a humor at once subtle and coarse, during which
the most unexpected things keep happening, notably
that attempt at *fugato*, serious and at the same time grotesque. We may ask, with Abert, if the last chords on
the strings, each string in a different key, may not be
interpreted as a final joke on the part of the performers
at the composer's expense—who truly, for all he had to
say, has kept them too long occupied.

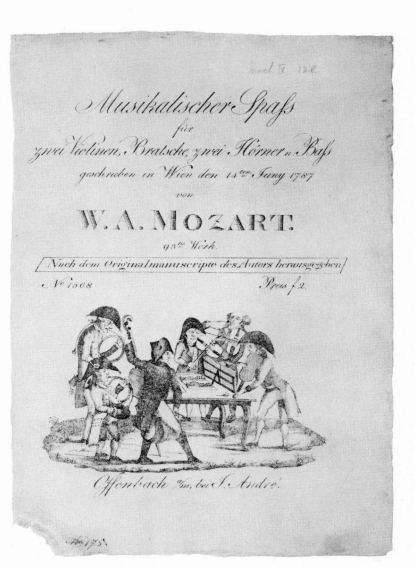

Title page of the first edition of 'A Musical Joke' (K. 522)

CHAPTER FOURTEEN

The Final Great Trilogy

SYMPHONY IN E FLAT
SYMPHONY IN G MINOR
SYMPHONY IN C (THE 'JUPITER')

W HEN ONE CONSIDERS THE level reached by Mozart at the time of writing *Don Giovanni*, one can say that he has there attained the most romantic summit of his entire career, since his three great symphonies all belong to this same period of artistic effort. *Don Giovanni* was first played at the end of October 1787, and the three symphonies were finished, one on June 26, 1788, and the others on July 25 and August 10 of the same year. We could, therefore, put the time of their inception in the first half of 1788. It would be not at all difficult to instance many a rhythmic or harmonic detail showing the three symphonies united to the famous opera by a common inspiration; and the scales that plow through the first page of the overture to the latter make their reappearance, with still bolder dissonances, in the spacious introduction to the E flat Symphony, the first of the three.[1]

In bestowing the title 'trilogy' on this famous set of

[1] See Abert: *W. A. Mozart*, Vol. II, p. 569.

masterpieces the suggestion of a bond between them is intentional; this trinity, we may be sure, has not come about by chance. Never since he arrived at maturity had he produced, at intervals of a few days only, a succession of compositions of the same caliber; the E flat Symphony represents an immense portico through which the composer reveals to us all the warm and poetic beauty thronging his mind, before surrendering himself before our eyes to a struggle of exalted passion, to be manifest in the Symphony in G minor; and finally he invites our presence at a sort of apotheosis of his musical genius, freed from all shackles, in what has come to be known as the 'Jupiter' Symphony. This imposing triple aspect that he gives to his symphonic testament in some measure sums up for us his inmost soul, and one can well understand that the production of the first should be followed so closely by the other two. But one surely ought not to imagine that Mozart intended to interpret all the vicissitudes he was going through at the time of writing; the sorry happenings of his daily round have nothing in common with the blossoming of his secret soul. And when all is said, it is to the hidden energy of his genius more than to any other cause that we must ascribe the creation of those three monumental works, dominating as they do his own instrumental work and, we may say, the whole of the instrumental output of the eighteenth century. As for the external circumstances attending on their birth, we are in total ignorance of them; we have not the least notion of the orchestra they were intended for,[2] nor any other particular detail of their origin or first public performance.

[2] The dates of the first editions, published by André of Offenbach, are: 1797, 1794, and 1793. (Tr.)

We must therefore be content, before embarking upon
an analysis, with a few critical sketches from France and
Germany dating from fifteen or twenty years after their
completion; that is to say, about the time when the
world first began to have some idea of their artistic importance and their pre-eminent beauty.

Mozart's instrumental music, principally his great
symphonies, began to make its appearance in France
from 1805 onwards, in the programs of the *Exercices
publics des élèves du Conservatoire*,' which were then
giving place to real concerts, with critical notices.[3] In
1806 a fragment of a Mozart symphony was received
'with enthusiasm,' and works of this master are so much
the fashion that the writer feels obliged to press for the
more frequent performance of Italian works: 'we have
even,' he writes with some indignation, 'had three pieces
by Mozart in the same concert.' On March 22, 1807 the
rehearsal of the Conservatoire pupils opened with a performance of a Mozart symphony, played this time in its
entirety; and we have good reason to believe the symphony in question to have been the G minor. 'If the
first movement, for example,' explains the writer, 'seems
to have less grandeur and, so to say, less ample proportions [than Haydn], there is more brilliance and light-
ness, though the harmony is as skillful and the modulations as bold. There is no andante of Haydn more enjoyable than this one by Mozart; in the second half a
new and quite original figure makes its appearance on
the basses alone, then is taken up by the other instruments with modulations, until the basses make use of
part of this figure to lead back to the first motif. This

[3] See *La Décade philosophique*, from 1805; *Les Tablettes*
(1810–11).

delightful theme is so well managed that, though the
movement is long, it seems to end too soon. The two
minuets are piquant and lively; and the final presto, a
movement sometimes a bit perfunctory in Haydn's symphonies, is here most charming. It is a *rondeau*,[4] both
melodic and at the same time full of spirit and warmth.
This is to dwell rather long on a single symphony; but
it is the first by this master to be heard at the Conservatoire for a long time (his overtures are another matter),
and what we said in our last number has tempted us to
go into these details.' [5] On April 5 following, a Mozart
symphony appeared again: 'The andante, from another
symphony, was a superlative choice and made a most
pleasing effect. The minuets, in lively tempo, and the
final presto were applauded as warmly as they were
played; and this warmth could only respond to a like
quality in the composition—a quite extraordinary
warmth, which one finds in all Mozart's best compositions. This master seems always to have written with
inspiration.' [6]

We cannot, unfortunately, determine with certainty
just which symphony was performed on April 19, 1807,
and which seems to absorb the critic in an ever growing
interest; perhaps it was the 'Jupiter': 'It is very difficult,
full of minute detail, of fleeting passages of imitation, of
fine nuances requiring from all the participants rare precision and sustained attention, with no relaxation whatever. This is especially true of the last presto, a brilliant
and satisfying movement when perfectly played, but

[4] All instrumental finales were apt to be called *rondeaux;* this
particular one has no connection with the rondo form.
[5] *La Décade philosophique:* 2nd Year, to September 1807. The
critical notices are due to La Chabeaussiere (1752–1820).
[6] Ibid.

which the least carelessness or inaccuracy would reduce
to chaos. Whether it be regarded as a virtue or a vice in
Mozart's music, this abundance of detail, of little subjects
and countersubjects scattered throughout the orchestra,
is a characteristic.[7] It is the excess, perhaps the abuse, of
a learned style and a fertile imagination. This music, despite its complication, is intelligible and even clear to
him who knows how to listen, provided nothing in the
execution is lacking; deprived of this degree of precision, so difficult to attain, you will understand nothing.'[8] And the Conservatoire students on May 24 gave
another performance, 'more glowing and accurate,' of
the G minor Symphony.

From this one can see how the French were struck by
their first contact with Mozart's instrumental art, and
it can even be said that the critic here shows himself infinitely more understanding and acute than when dealing with Mozartian opera, whether *Les Mystères d'Isis*
(1801) or *Don Giovanni* (1805). Theorists, too, were
not inactive, and the G minor was made the subject of a
long critical analysis—or rather corrective, for the author is profoundly shocked by the liberties, particularly
in the harmony, that Mozart permits himself—signed
J. de Momigny.[9] I shall naturally ignore the corrections
that the author, in the name of 'good taste,' suggests in
almost every bar of the symphony, but retain his æsthetic appreciation of the general character of the first
movement, the first subject of which is 'of an impassioned grief.' Likewise in the second part of the finale

[7] Perhaps, indeed, the fugal finale of the 'Jupiter' is here in
question.
[8] Ibid.
[9] Framery et Guinguené: *Encyclopédie méthodique*, Vol. III,
art. *"Symphonie,"* pp. 412 ff. (1818).

—that is to say, during the course of the development—
we are in the presence of an 'eloquent frenzy of a lost,
tormented soul, but perhaps Mozart has counted too
much on the intelligence of the players. . . .' As for the
andante, 'we see there only magnificent accompani-
ments, and we seek the countenance of this grand and
handsome body. . . .'

When we compare these pre-romantic criticisms with
those of thirty-five years or more ago, we can realize the
changes that have taken·place between our great-grand-
fathers' generation and that of our fathers or our own.
The G minor Symphony toward the end of the nineteenth century is scarcely more than a musical trifle
tinged with gentle melancholy. What would have been
said then of a writer daring to speak of '*l'éloquent délire*'
of Mozart? Mozart is invariably Apollo, or at least a
Parthenon frieze. And his admirers of twenty or thirty
years ago would have been almost grieved had one
spoken of the ardent passion, the warm tenderness,
which almost every page of Mozart holds for us.

Passing now to German criticism at the beginning of
the nineteenth century, we encounter some very.similar
appraisals; as in France, it is most often the G minor
Symphony whose passionate ardor calls forth comment.
At the Augarten subscription concerts in Vienna, in
existence since Mozart's time, the G minor Symphony
was heard in 1804: 'this veritable masterpiece where
nothing is too long or too short, where all is conducted
in the most exact fashion; where everything down to the
finest detail contributes to the whole and seems indispensable to the completion of the mighty picture of a
mind swayed by passion, ranging from the extremity of
grief to the borders of the sublime. However often the

work is heard, it never fails in its effect; every time it
grips the listener irresistibly and sweeps him along in its
train.' ¹⁰ Nearly a year later, in May 1805, there is another performance of this amazing symphony at the
same concerts. 'This symphony which combines the
highest beauty with the greatest nobility of inspiration,
and, moreover, founders neither in violence nor in
bizarrerie.' It is a colossal canvas preserving the most
exquisite proportions; 'a Jupiter from the chisel of a
Phidias, inspiring both respect and love.' ¹¹ In another
performance during the same year the minuet seems to
have been omitted; and the critic exclaims: 'what a pity
to suppress the terribly beautiful minuet!' ¹²

The impression made on all the writers of the time
seems to have been one of tragic grandeur, to which we
had not been accustomed by romantic criticism. And in
1808 we come across this conclusion: 'This symphony
in which the composer tears so powerfully at our heart-
strings that they resound interminably.' ¹³

The E flat Symphony occasions quite a poem from
the pen of the critic Apel, and if the name *Jupiter* inter-
venes in an unexpected fashion to underline Mozart's last
symphony, it is because everyone is agreed in finding in
it the apogee of power and grandeur; but it should be
noted that in both France and Germany criticism becomes more readily expansive over the exalted passion
which, for them and ourselves likewise, is the core of
the Symphony in G minor.¹⁴

¹⁰ *Allgemeine Musikalische-Zeitung,* Vol. VI (1804), p. 777.
¹¹ *Allgemeine Musikalische-Zeitung,* Vol. VII, p. 502.
¹² Ibid., p. 613.
¹³ Ibid., 1808, p. 239.
¹⁴ After the analysis of each of these three great Mozart symphonies I shall continue to give a review of the criticisms they

Symphony in E Flat

Completed June 26, 1788

The scoring consists of strings (cello and bass parts distinct), one flute, two clarinets, two bassoons, two horns, two trumpets, and drums.

*64—K.543

Immediately following this solemn rhythmic attack a descending scale, in thirty-second notes, is given to the violins, with an ascending motif on the flute, while underneath, the timpani maintain a continuous roll. These scales will streak the whole introduction, and from the violins they pass to the basses, where, in contrast, their direction is upwards. And always, beneath these varied scale passages, the persistent, jerky rhythm is maintained, first by the basses, then by the trumpets:

*65

have evoked. Beginning at the end of the eighteenth century, we shall run quickly through much of the nineteenth century, ending about 1870, paying more particular attention to the appreciations of such men as Fétis, Hector Berlioz, and Richard Wagner.

suggesting almost irresistibly an analogous passage in the slow introduction to the *Don Giovanni* overture:

*66

The harmonic boldness of the last measures of the introduction:

*67

gives to the whole of the E flat Symphony a romantic character, which will be apparent in each of the four movements.

*68

This theme, smooth, warm, and sensuous, is followed later by a powerful ritornello, with a sort of gypsy rhythm:

*69

then, exactly as in the introduction, descending scales
reappear on the violins:

*70

considerably lengthening the ritornello. The second
subject, in B flat, is divided between the violins and the
woodwind:

*71

which, for four measures, are supported simply by the
basses; the second part of this second subject itself makes
a third subject:

*72

allotted to the strings, accompanied, or punctuated, by
double basses pizzicato. Then comes a much extended
and developed version of the ritornello that followed
the first subject, fresh modulations making the return
of the gypsy rhythm on the violins still more incisive.
The end of the first ritornello thus serves as a conclusion
of the first part of the movement.

After the double bar the development opens with modulations based on the final group of this ritornello, giving place to a repeat of the second part of the second subject (Ex.72) in A flat, still with the same pizzicato accompaniment. The final group that ushered in the development reappears, giving rise to modulating imitations between basses and first violins; then comes the second subject ritornello, varied and modulated. This is arrested on the dominant of C minor; there is a whole measure's silence, then the woodwind alone, in three measures, effects a join (analogous to that at the end of the introduction) with an unexpected modulation.

*73

The recapitulation follows the exposition closely, and the movement ends with a brilliant coda, with no separating repeat marks. The concluding rhythm is very nearly identical with that of the close of the first part.

*74

This theme, which some have found flat and insipid, is going to transport us into unimagined regions, and its faintly martial character hardly prepares us for all the vicissitudes, fierce or gentle, that will arise from its development.

Note first that it is presented by the strings alone, cellos quite distinct from the double basses—thus helping to give the whole movement a romantic character, a modern flavor. The theme is binary in form; it is furnished with repeat marks and a recapitulation, but on its last appearance there is a modulation to the minor. After another double bar line the woodwinds, as in the first movement, provide a link to the first episode (in F minor). This:

*75

is almost explosive in its energy and abruptness, as Mozart's minor episodes very often are. During the course of this episode the first subject somewhat unexpectedly reappears, in imitation between bassoons and horns on the one hand, and violas and basses on the other. The ascending rhythm of the first subject continues in the bass, slurred, while the violins are concerned with a detached, descending figure, forte, in opposition. A remarkable transition in the first violins leads to a third subject or episode, piano, on the woodwind accompanied by the violins:

*76

This third subject is repeated, in imitations between flutes, clarinets, and bassoons, supported by a sustained

chord on the horns. The return of the initial theme then
follows, but from the fifth measure it passes to the
woodwind, violins weaving an expressive counter-
melody around it; then the basses and first violins divide
the theme between them, with descending scales on the
woodwind. The latter then take charge of the theme,
while the violins again adorn it with the counter-melody
just mentioned; and the minor version of the theme
leads, by a marvelous modulation, to the key of B major
and the repeat of the first episode, more energetic than
ever, this time in B minor. This reprise is extended by
some new modulations, as expressive as they are unexpected, testifying to a sort of romantic exaltation; the
other themes follow in their appropriate order, and then
comes a fine coda on the principal theme, initiated by
antiphony between woodwind and strings; and the
movement, after some expressive and languorous chromaticisms, comes to an end on two chords, forte, by the
whole orchestra.

*77

This minuet, the most popular of all in Mozart's
works, seems to spring from a single idea; and rhythms
from the development section of the first movement will
be clearly heard. It deploys the full orchestra, and its
lively and energetic movement is pursued in one single
sweep to the end. The customary contrast arises from
the quiet tenderness of the trio:

*78

in the same key; the first clarinet states the theme to the accompaniment of the second, to which the flute replies with a delicate echo. This trio, quite German or Austrian in character, belongs to the same genre as Mozart's last German dances, a genre very similar to that adopted by Schubert in his waltzes and *Ländler*. The trio might well figure in one of the many dance suites composed by Mozart between 1788 and 1791, for the balls and assemblies of Vienna. The compositions his duties obliged him to provide gave him the opportunity to crowd these little pieces, alas, too little known, with gems of orchestration belonging essentially to the symphony. The study of these orchestral suites even throws a new light on the symphonic art of the master, now nearing the end of his short life.

*79

The first violins alone state the theme, accompanied by the seconds. Then the whole orchestra attacks the theme, quickly followed by long roulades, brilliant and gay, on the violins, carried on through a whole page of the score, leading to a fanfare-like cadence in F major. This separates the first period of the second subject, which is itself none other than a return to the first subject—but how varied! The sly and melancholy response of the woodwind is succeeded by modulations becoming more and more audacious and distant, the fanfare rhythms are renewed, and everything halts abruptly on a six-four chord. It might be imagined that the ritornello ended there; but now the woodwinds become involved in some rapid imitations based on the opening of the first subject, and the first half of the movement comes to an end with a loud and joyous ritornello, in B flat, on the fanfare rhythm previously noted. At the double bar it becomes apparent that the rhythm of the first subject is going to be pursued throughout the whole of this remarkable finale; Mozart, in fact, here returns to the principle of construction he had adopted in 1786. He built his instrumental movements on a single theme, reserving the right to treat and vary it at his pleasure. So at the double bar the strings attack the first notes of the main theme, in unison, in the dominant of C minor, with all the roughness usual with Mozart when he goes into the minor key. But a bar's rest modifies to some extent the violence of this opening of the development; the theme appears in the violins exactly as at the beginning of the movement, but this time in A flat. The first measures of the theme give rise to an extraordinary development that maintains its rhythm throughout, while the theme is made to pass through inspired modulations beginning in the most distant key (E major); it is exchanged between first violins and basses during nine measures, and then, with imitations at a closer interval in the same measure, the first and second violins range themselves against the violas and basses. The contest is so exhausting that the theme disintegrates, after a violent unison in G; the fragments continue to appear in the

violins, while the woodwinds are busy right up to the
recapitulation, with phrases that defy description:

*80

The latter is regular, with thirteen bars of frenzied coda
ending, à la Haydn, with the initial rhythm of the movement.

Everyone is agreed in recognizing in this symphony
as it were the full flowering of the happiness an artist
feels in creation. It seems to me, however, that there are
plenty of signs of trouble and uneasiness; the spontaneous audacity of the harmonies Mozart piles up in the
introduction, above the dull murmur of those pregnant
scale passages, is scarcely a fitting prelude to a cloudless
day. For us this introduction stands at the threshold of
a new era; it has a dominating grandeur presaging Beethoven; [15] there is, in Haydn at least, no parallel symphonic opening. It is a new starting-point and, being
something tremendous said for the first time, cannot fail
to excite some measure of astonishment. Mozart, as I
have already remarked, here recaptures very fleetingly
the accents of his *Don Giovanni* overture; nor will this
be the sole instance in the three symphonies when we
shall experience his brusque boldness. Then, the allegro
theme comes rather as a relief after the heavy atmos-

[15] See Abert: *W. A. Mozart*, Vol. II, pp. 568 ff., where he
speaks of 'profound pessimism.'

phere of the prelude. It is the cantabile type of allegro frequent in Mozart and very characteristic of him. But its division between strings and woodwind, its soft, shaded light, peculiar to the key of E flat, the advantage derived from the use of the clarinet, all go to produce an astonishingly novel effect and, if we add to this a gypsy touch, an impression quite unknown in the music of the time; we have no hesitation in labeling it with that over-worked term *romantic*. The development, it is true, has nothing of the fullness it will acquire in the remaining two symphonies; but the contrast provoked by the op-position and the key changes of the three subjects ac-centuates the romantic character of the work. Counter-point does not here play the preponderant role we are accustomed to in the classical symphony; but the com-poser includes in the development nothing that is not strictly thematic and—a new proof of the æsthetic and expressive importance of key in Mozart's work—there are to be found, toward the end, some characteristic ef-fects exactly similar to those in the development section of his famous Piano Concerto in C minor (first move-ment), produced by the same means, and by modulation to the same keys.

All through the symphony the harmonic aspect should stand out in relief, since this is largely instru-mental in giving a romantic feeling and attitude to the whole. At the moment toward the end of the develop-ment when the whole orchestra comes to rest on a pause, followed by the woodwind link passage built on sevenths and ninths, we are in the presence of innovations prob-ably without precedent; and this procedure not only appears new, but was so intended by the composer, since the introduction is joined to the allegro by similar means.

And it would not be difficult to instance other harmonic audacities in the andante and the finale.

This andante exhibits a curious peculiarity in the choice of the key of A flat. The choice is romantic in itself; and the unexpected sequence of the episodes unfolded therein makes it a movement unique of its kind. But, once more confirming my thesis of the importance of key to Mozart, we find the same harmonic surprises, if not the same inspiration, in the extraordinary adagio that forms the second movement of a Sonata in E flat, for piano and violin, composed by Mozart toward the end of 1785.[16] We must expect every kind of surprise when Mozart leads us into the almost forbidden territory of A flat. In the andante under discussion, when the theme sounds in the principal key, it awakens in us grave and calm echoes, almost always veiled; but this mysterious region does not remain unchanged; it is sometimes illuminated as by a lightning flash, returning to its former state only after heavy and plaintive lamentations. There is nothing more expressive than this return after the furious outburst of the first episode; the elegiac and tender intimacy of the whole movement is fully revealed only after the various episodes, when in the coda the first theme becomes even more penetrating, its expression more touching and intense. Its sway is exerted more especially in the chromaticisms, which in one or two measures give a greater poignancy to the principal subject, without destroying the slightly repressed character that persists almost throughout the andante.

[16] K.481. The adagio of the string Trio in E flat, nearly contemporaneous with the symphony, could also be quoted for its boldness.

All this is very complex, and even the two almost cruel chords ending the movement provide a new matter for astonishment; for everything had seemed to point to a quiet ending to this elegy, despite the sharply energetic outbursts running through it.

The finale has more surprises prepared for us, of which we are scarcely forewarned by its sprightly and good-natured theme. This, as I have already said, comprises the one and only subject of the movement; more marvelous still, out of it Mozart builds a world whose significance I have no hesitation in saying is, if not greater, at least more original than that of the first movement. One can find many passages having symmetrical equivalents in the first movement (a fact that gives to many of Mozart's works such a complete unity), and especially some enharmonic modulations which, with the changing color of a single note, open up a new world,[17] a procedure and result essentially romantic. Then there is the truly ineffable passage preceding the recapitulation, when the theme crumbles and disintegrates after its struggle with itself, while the woodwind, in keys as remote as possible, transport us toward the unknown regions. In truth, here is not 'woodwind,' but the wind itself,[18] a murmuring breeze, a zephyr from so distant a poetry that it defies description! The general exuberance with which this finale overflows (reminding us of Haydn) is not all, for Mozart has such a strong tendency toward poetic fantasy that he finds the opportunity, always and everywhere, even in the midst of the

[17] See, for example, the change from A flat to E major in the development.

[18] *'ce ne sont plus des "vents," mais le vent.'*

most boisterous festivities, to insinuate something of a self-revelatory nature, charged with tenderness and emotion.[19]

The learned Fétis, two years after the inauguration of his *Revue musicale*, gives an account (April 27, 1828),[20] of a concert 'composed entirely of the works of Mozart.'

'The symphony that was chosen to open the first part was the E flat. It contains much beauty, particularly in the adagio and the finale; but I must confess I felt some astonishment at seeing it preferred to the G minor, that beautiful and passionate composition! The latter was deemed too well known; but the overture to *Die Zauberflöte* is still more so, and we saw the effect that produced. The E flat Symphony has not the brilliance we expect after the grand effects of Beethoven's symphonies. There are no parts for the oboes, because at the time Mozart wrote it oboists played in that key only with considerable difficulty, regarding it as too arduous. I do not know if the somewhat unfavorable opinion a section of the orchestra had of this work had undermined their morale, but it seemed to me that the performance had less sureness and precision than in other concerts, and even in the remainder of this one.'

The opinion here expressed by Fétis seems to have been modified but little as time went on. In one of the last articles written by the great Berlioz for the *Gazette musicale*, in which he was responsible for concert notices, we find these few hasty lines sufficing to describe

[19] The sketch of another Symphony in E flat also begins with a slow introduction. (K. Anh. 100.)

[20] *Revue musicale*, p. 318.

the symphony: 'The concert ended with the E flat Symphony by Mozart. With the exception of the last movement, truly unworthy of such a master, this symphony by the charm of its melodies seems to surpass by far that by Haydn (no. 30) (?) which we have just quoted. It was, however, much less applauded!' (February 13, 1842.)

So the success of this symphony, so intimately Mozartian, remained a qualified one. It has neither the passion of the G minor nor the imposing splendor of the 'Jupiter'; therefore neither public nor critics of the romantic age were capable of being profoundly moved by it. A symphony at that time had perforce to be powerful or mournful throughout. We shall see in due course that certain minuets were barely tolerated. At the same time the caustic and almost clownish wit of many a Haydn finale began to offend the ear profoundly. It is likely that the character of the theme of the finale of the E flat Symphony was the cause of the severity of its condemnation; the beauty of the treatment of this unique subject could not compensate for the impression the theme itself produced. What we have noticed as precisely 'romantic' in the course of this symphony, and even in this very finale, was completely overlooked. It is more astonishing that the bold and imposing introduction, stirring up dark depths—an opening on the whole much more impressive and romantic than that of either of the two following symphonies—does not seem to have aroused any comment. Most curiously, this abridged model for the prelude of Beethoven's Seventh Symphony, with its forceful scales, its already sinister and uneasy harmonies, makes no impression. And it is not the absence of oboes that caused musicians, critics,

the public, to have an unfavorable opinion of the E flat
Symphony, which with the recoil of time we regard as
one of those in which Mozart's genius is affirmed with
the most original variety, with the most unfettered
fancy, and above all with youthful and intense poetry.

Speaking generally, the romantic epoch was satisfied
with nothing but enormous ensembles in instrumental
music. This megalomania swamped chamber music.
Mozart's, wholly scorned, was relegated to programs of
the second order. And Berlioz expressed very clearly
the state of mind that obtained right to the end of the
century when he said, apropos of a concert given by the
Société des Concerts du Conservatoire, of Beethoven's
F major Symphony: 'It is colossal. Frankly, however
one regards it, it is folly to attempt any comparison between such a symphony and those of Mozart, even the
finest; the contest is unequal.' [21]

Some thirty years later another genius illuminates
with an astonishing penetration the masterpieces of an
art already become classic, which on this account had
to suffer from an inflexible 'tradition,' established, it is
true, long after the composer's death. Here is how, early
in 1865, Richard Wagner complains with bitterness, in
a report addressed to the King of Bavaria, of the absence
of any authoritative direction with regard to the interpretation of Mozart's orchestral works in Germany: [22]

'Now, let us imagine some such expressive theme of
Mozart's—Mozart, who was intimately acquainted with
the noble style of classical Italian singing, whose musical

[21] *Gazette musicale*, March 27, 1836.
[22] Richard Wagner: *Bericht . . . über eine in München zu er-
richtende deutsche Musikschule* (English translation by Edward
Dannreuther): "On a German School of Music."

expression derived its very soul from the delicate vibra-
tions, swellings and accents of that style, and who was
the first to reproduce the effects of this vocal style, by
means of orchestral instruments. Let us imagine such a
theme of the master's played neatly and smoothly, by
an instrument in the orchestra, without any inflection, or
increase or decrease of tone or accent, without the
slightest touch of that modification of movement and
rhythm so indispensable to good singing—but monot-
onously enunciated, just as one might pronounce some
arithmetical number—and then, let us endeavour to form
a conclusion as to the vast difference between the master's original intention, and the impressions thus produced. The dubious value of the veneration of Mozart,
professed by our musical traditionalists will then also
appear. To show this more distinctly, let us examine a
particular case—for example, the first eight bars of the
second movement of Mozart's celebrated symphony in
E flat. Take this beautiful theme as it appears on paper,
with hardly any marks of expression; fancy it played
smoothly and complacently, as the score apparently has
it—and compare the result with the manner in which a
true musician would feel and sing it! How much of
Mozart does this theme convey, if played, as in nine
cases out of ten it *is* played, in a perfectly colourless and
lifeless way? "Poor pen and paper music, without a
shadow of soul or sense." '

From all this the significance for Richard Wagner of
this E flat Symphony, and especially the 'marvelous
theme' with which it opens, is plainly to be seen. It is
not my purpose here to point the moral for orchestral
conductors, but to stress Wagner's choice of this symphonic fragment, out of the whole of Mozart's output,

to try to convince us of the necessity of 'singing tone' in rendering Mozart. Previously he had pointed out the almost complete absence of directions in Mozart's symphonies; he assumes that the master must have given them himself by word of mouth in conducting his works, thus making himself better understood to his interpreters.

'But the precise importance of these [expression marks] for the performance of Mozart's instrumental works is obvious. With Mozart the so-called development sections, and the connecting links between the main themes, are frequently rather slight, whereas his musical originality shows to greatest advantage in the vocal character of the melodies. Compared with Haydn's the significance of Mozart's symphonies lies in the extraordinarily expressive vocal character of his instrumental themes; it is in this character that we find the explanation of how Mozart, in this branch of music, was a great creator.' [23]

It was not chance, but his own genius, that prompted Wagner's choice of the E flat Symphony to illustrate the difference between the performance of this symphony under the direction of an inspired artist and the indifferent interpretations, colorless and lifeless, giving the impression of 'soulless music,' that we are usually offered. The finale seems to him quite as important as the first movement. He sees in it a very eloquent example of those allegros wherein the figuration outweighs the melody. 'It is,' he adds, 'an orgy of pure rhythm.' [24] These famous words of Wagner apply as much to the

[23] Ibid.
[24] Richard Wagner: *Über das Dirigiren* (English translation, *The Art of Conducting,* by Edward Dannreuther).

finale of Beethoven's Seventh Symphony as to that of Mozart's E flat; these movements are, for him, equal in value.

This, moreover, is not the first time this similarity has impressed itself on Wagner's mind. In one of the most charming passages from his memoirs, entitled: *"Ein glücklicher Abend,"* we read the following:

'. . . We had, among other lovely things, Mozart's E flat and Beethoven's Seventh.

'. . . In my opinion there is always this difference between these two symphonies: in Mozart the language of the heart is breathed in quiet and tender longing, while in the work of his rival this desire is hurled boldly toward the infinite. In Mozart's symphony it is the plenitude of feeling that is uppermost; in Beethoven's, the fearless consciousness of power.

' "How I love," cried my friend, "to hear you thus illumining these sublime orchestral compositions!" ' [25]

Quite clearly these two works are on an equal footing in Wagner's admiration, and it is not difficult to discover in the shrewd and involved prose of the composer of *Tristan* many a phrase inspired by a common profound passion for the two great pioneers of the symphony.

Symphony in G Minor

Completed July 25, 1788

The scoring was originally, besides strings (cellos and basses), one flute, two oboes, two bassoons, and two horns. Later Mozart replaced the two oboes by two clarinets, while two oboes were added with modified

[25] Ibid.

parts. There are no trumpets or drums. The sharp tang of the original oboes must have tended to heighten the true character of the work.

*81—K.550.

With no introduction or preparation at all the composer plunges right into his subject, hasty and uneasy. The theme is stated by the violins alone, and is accompanied by *divisi* violas. On the second statement the woodwinds add some sustained chords; and the sequel to the first subject—really a second subject already, in B flat—reaches the forte level. It is impossible to imagine a clearer demarcation between the constituent subjects of the movement: the true second subject, indisputably Mozartian in its chromaticisms, is in fact stated, by strings alone, only after a complete measure's rest:

*82

the response is by the oboes and clarinets,[26] and on the second subject being repeated the scoring is interchanged; this time it is stated by the woodwind, strings replying. Then a modulating ritornello of energetic

[26] Clarinets and bassoons in 'Philharmonia' miniature score. (Tr.)

character, opening piano, in A flat, brings us again to
the rhythm of the first subject, in a coda, which is twice
repeated, to conclude, after a brilliant ritornello in unison, in B flat. A single chord before the double bar
brings the first part to an abrupt close.

The same slashing chord is again twice repeated, by
the whole orchestra, to open the development section.
With an abrupt stroke of genius these two chords have
served to lead us into the key farthest removed from
that of the movement (F-sharp minor): the principal
theme accordingly appears in this key, with sustained
chords on the woodwind:

After modulations and extensions it reappears in the
basses in the key of E minor, under a new and very energetic figure on the violins; then, in a forceful and magnificent expansion, the basses and violins alternate,
bandying the principal subject and the eighth-note figure in a vigorous development:

*84

The woodwinds have sustained chords, and the bassoon doubles the bass. The principal subject persists in the violins, while the woodwinds present a modified version in counterpoint with it. Very soon the latter respond with the first two eighth notes of the theme only. A dialogue follows, with this fragment of the initial theme, broken up and as if rolled out, tossed back and forth in contrary motion and with a feverish haste between the basses and the violins. Then the woodwinds, unattended, embark on the transition passage designed to lead up to the recapitulation, a phrase whose descending chromaticisms give rise to poignantly expressive modulations:

*85

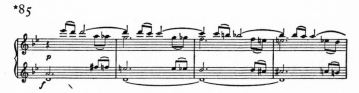

It will be seen that the development is strictly thematic. The recapitulation is at first identical; but what I have called the sequel to the first subject now gives rise to what is a veritable second development in counterpoint between the first violins and the basses, with the second violins continuing the eighth-note figure. This sequel to the first subject then reappears, victorious, in the principal key. The same measure's silence, as in the first part, divides the second subject from the foregoing; it is now in the tonic, giving it much more intensity of expression; the layout is the same as on its first appearance, but its continuation undergoes an expressive extension. A coda (not separated by double bars, and based entirely

on the opening measures of the theme) sums up ener-
getically and concentrates in a few measures all the expression of this first movement:

*86

an expression that in the last pages takes on a wild and
excited character, only to sink back finally into a feeling
of resigned lassitude.

*87

This is to some extent but an outline, opening in
counterpoint with the basses and employing at first only
the string quartet; on its repetition a counter-melody
soars above in the violins. The austere bareness of this
opening, which is to serve as a basis for a song of unsuspected beauty, is immediately suggestive of Bach. From
the first violins the second half of this first subject is
transferred to the bass, and out of this continuation
springs a rising motif of two thirty-second notes, which
will permeate the entire movement. It is first woven
around the melodic phrase that closes this double exposition of the principal subject in the tonic, now ascending, now descending. It is impossible to overestimate the

importance of the basses in all this andante, an importance that Mozart will stress perhaps still more in the
andante of the next symphony: we have here as it were
a presentiment of what is to come later.

The second subject, separated as in the first movement, is attacked forte, in B flat, while its response, constructed out of the aforementioned figure, is heard on
the flute and the oboes [27] and concludes in F major. The
main theme of the movement then reappears, in D flat,
still in counterpoint on the strings, and occasions some
bold modulations, while above its implacable solidity the
airy thirty-second notes, now in a descending figure,
drop like pearls from the woodwind, glistening and
shimmering over these dark depths; the whole clears at
last, leading to a cadence, forte, in the dominant.[28] A
naïve and unexpected response, forming a third subject,
emerges in the strings, as a coda:

*88

It is soon followed by modulations as bold as the preceding ones, making the ritornello that concludes the first

[27] Clarinets in 'Philharmonia' miniature score. (Tr.)
[28] Robert Schumann has remarked that the repeat of the theme
in D flat, exactly similar, arises from an error: four measures
ought to be omitted in both the first and the second parts; and
this is confirmed by an examination of the original autograph.
These measures are, in the first part, measures 29 to 32, and in the
second, measures 48 to 51. See Robert Schumann: *Gesammelte
Schriften*, Vol. II, p. 32.

part, in which both strings and wind are employed, even
more thoroughly Mozartian and angelic.

The development has few equals in expressive depth,
even in the works of Mozart. It opens with the rhythm
of the principal subject on a unison C flat. To this persistently grave and heavy rhythm is joined the little
thirty-second-note figure that, as I have already said,
pervades all the andante, now cascading from the wind
instruments, now gliding from the strings; before finally
arriving at the dominant of C minor it runs through the
most varied keys; and the return of the principal subject, in C minor, in the woodwind, is first effected by a
descending chromatic scale. Over this first subject is
now erected a new chromatic figure of an elegiac character, quite 'Wagnerian' and ultra-expressive:

*89

It is so modern and poignant in character, in its brevity,
that its role could not be restricted to that of a simple
transition destined to lead back to the recapitulation;
Mozart felt it so strongly that he used it again in this
recapitulation in a guise perhaps even more expressive:

*90

Notice, too, that it is merely a transposition of the second measure of the initial theme. From the recapitulation of the first subject in G flat the continuation of the astonishing procession is reproduced before our eyes with hardly any changes save those occasioned by its transposition into the main key of the movement.

*91

In spite of the heading *Allegretto* the character of the whole of the minuet is suggestive of a bitter and merciless struggle. The rugged counterpoint of the old masters becomes here the most efficient vehicle of, as it were, a paroxysm of nervous tension. Twice during the second half the counterpoint is renewed: the minuet theme attacked by the basses after the double bar descends by steps of a third, after which the trebles drag it violently toward the heights; then, following the energetic cadence chords, we have the first measures of the theme, transfigured, given out piano by the woodwind alone, they being perhaps better designed to set off the unique moment of sunshine that is the trio (in the major):

*92

Calm, reposeful, pellucid, truly idyllic! The charming curves of the theme are outlined by strings alone, with the response on the woodwind; and in all the second part of this trio the alternation of strings and wind enact an episode so pure and calm, of so Elysian a grace, that in a few bars the tragic adventure of the whole symphony has been obliterated from our minds. Here, exactly as in the first minuet, Mozart, with the sole idea of creating a bond of profound unity between the two, leaves the wind with a short solo passage a few bars before the end.

*93

The allegro assai opens, with an impetuous and demoniac speed, with a theme that, with its refrain:

*94

extends for 32 measures; its double exposition is ensured by repeat marks. The refrain is followed by a long theme in eighth notes, stated first by the violins, then in imitations between the violins and the basses. The impression gained is of a constant opposition between *soli* and *tutti*. Exactly as in the first movement, to which the finale offers some striking similarities, the second subject is clearly separated from the first:

*95

The exposition is entrusted to strings alone, piano, and is then passed to the woodwind, varied (melodically and harmonically) and broadened; there is a return to the violin ritornello in company with imitations of the opening. As we have again a movement in sonata form, this section ends conclusively with big chords in B flat, followed by a double bar line.

The development is perhaps of all his work the one wherein Mozart shows the highest degree of passion and even fury. All the resources of his art, rhythm, harmony, counterpoint, are carried to extremes; a contorted, demoniac force has seized him, nor is the listener granted any respite. It is an unusual crisis made manifest by a stroke of genius. Such boldnesses indicate a paroxysm of exaltation, and not free artistic creation. There is no more liberty here, but a mad constraint that seems to leave the composer with not an atom of air to breathe. And despite the severity of such a paroxysm—and this is really the core of the Mozartian miracle—neither the characteristic beauty of the work nor its proportions suffer the least injury, nor is the course of the ideas harmed by such violent and cruel shocks.

With Mozart's customary abruptness in a like case, this development opens with the first subject attacked in the key of B-flat minor:

*96

then, after a few notes interspersed with rests, the theme
is attacked anew, on the dominants of D minor, G minor, C minor, and F minor. Canonic imitations appear,
first on the flute, then on the bassoon; and now we see a
grand *fugato* breaking out among the strings.

One cannot too strongly call attention to this page, in
which all the contrapuntal force and the prodigious im-
petus of which the theme shows itself capable are concentrated.

*97

From the point of view of rhythm and harmony, also
from the richness and unexpected variety of its modulations, it seems no exaggeration to say that this *fugato* is
one of the monuments of all music; the way the general
mood of the movement—of fury and almost delirious
exaltation—is strengthened and fortified by its audacious freedom seems to me a transmutation of the technique of the older music to the most 'modern' ends.
After a page of combat the imitations, instead of being
confined to strings, are exchanged between the woodwind and basses. Both woodwind and basses have a role

of capital importance difficult to overestimate. It is they alone, the wind, who, after the few bars intercalated with rests with which this quasi-volcanic development opens, unlock the floodgates releasing this musical torrent. So we may say, as the struggle is intensified, so the clashes between wind and basses are exercised in the sharper keys, those furthest removed from the key of the movement, while imperious and somber horn-calls re-echo.[29]

This persists for two whole pages of the score, with insistent repetitions and a growing boldness, until the struggle is terminated at last on a chord of the diminished seventh.

The recapitulation is at first exact, save for the omission of the second exposition of the principal subject; but the second subject, though not lengthened, is varied. More, its expressive intensity is multiplied tenfold by being cast in G minor, a tonality that for Mozart always bore a marked significance of passionate feverishness. The conclusion also is similar; but by the word *conclusion* I mean the very last measures, for the final ritornello is extended by several measures that moreover contain no hint of appeasement or resignation. An almost furious transport of rage persists, with no relenting; we can say that here Mozart exhausts the musical possibilities of such a feeling, and that too without departing from the principal subject, on which, in fact, the whole of the development has been based.

While the first movement offers some respite and, toward the end, a sort of resigned lassitude, there is no place here for such lulls; a raging torrent bursts its banks,

[29] It is a bit difficult to follow M. Saint-Foix here, since the horns are silent during the whole of this passage. (Tr.)

uprooting trees and upheaving boulders. Only the second subject, which with its chromaticisms is but a
heartrending plaint when it reappears just before the
end, succeeds in interrupting the storm for a few measures only, after which the flood's fury is redoubled and
finally sweeps all before it.

The G minor Symphony, as I have said already, is the
symphony that has occasioned the most characteristic
and the greatest number of commentaries. With such a
work one is almost justified in saying that these commentaries constitute interpretations. Also I feel bound
to quote some of them, with their exact dates, so that
the reader can at least estimate the changes wrought by
the passage of time when the interpretation of a work
of art is in question. The evolution of criticism through
the ages seems to me one of the studies most worthy of
the attention of the historian.

We know that the Chevalier de Nissen, the second
husband of Mozart's widow, busied himself conscien-
tiously in collecting material for a life of Mozart: he has
left us, not a life, but only the material for one. The
following passage is extracted from this (1828):

'We notice the G minor Symphony, which offers in
its four movements the expression of a restless and uneasy passion, a struggle, a contest with a forcefully penetrating agitation; we notice the E flat Symphony,
wherein the language is calmer, wherein is no subject
for tears, no inconsolable grief, but rather a passion il-
lumined by many a ray of heavenly hope.' [30]

During the same year, 1828, Fétis, in his new *Revue
musicale* (May 11), sums up his impressions of the G

[30] Nissen: *Biographie de Mozart*, p. 159.

minor Symphony, which had been performed at one of
the Duchess de Berry's concerts:

'Although Mozart in this symphony has not been
lavish in his orchestral demands, although those mass effects that astonish and transport us in the Beethoven
symphonies will not be found here, the inventive fire
burning in this work, the passionate and energetic tones
there poured out, the melancholy hue which prevails,
make of it one of the very finest productions of the human mind.'

Later, in writing his article on Mozart in his *Biographie des musiciens*, he does not hesitate to declare the
G minor Symphony as 'the discovery of a new world of
music.' [31]

If now we turn to the criticism of 'young France' we
find ourselves in a noticeably different atmosphere.
What Hector Berlioz finds most striking in such a work
as the G minor is first of all the grace, delicacy, and
charm of the melodies, the detail of the workmanship;
there is no question of melancholy, still less of passion.
There is little between this mode of appreciation and
Robert Schumann's, who apropos of this symphony in-
vokes Apollo and the impassive beauty of the Greek
temple. But let us follow Berlioz through his years as
critic of the *Gazette musicale*.

March 6, 1836: 'Mozart's Symphony in G minor, that
model of delicacy and naïveté, rendered this time exactly in the style best suited to it, conquered even the
most exclusive admirers of Beethoven; the minuet had
to be repeated. It would be hard, in truth, to hear anything more charming in grace and loveliness than the
trio of this movement; and even were it deprived of the

[31] Fétis, op. cit., Vol. VI, p. 243.

spell of such perfect playing it would, I believe, never fail in its effect.'

April 9, 1840: 'G minor Symphony, Mozart. First movement admirably fashioned and full of charming fancies; adagio tender, quiet, calm, and delicate; the minuet, vigorous opening, deliciously graceful and naïve in the middle; the finale full of verve, strewn with fragments of adorable melody.'

Finally, February 28, 1841: 'Mozart's G minor Symphony opened the proceedings; it is very melodious, very distinguished, very delicately wrought; the trio of the minuet especially is a masterpiece of naïve grace which could scarcely be surpassed. I say the trio, for the minuet itself ranks for me among the sort of broad jokes I spoke of the other day in connection with Haydn.'

We have here a very widespread opinion among the average audience, and a most persistent one. Fifty years later it will have changed scarcely at all. We see that listening to a symphony has become a serious matter; Haydn laughed too much, or tried to make us laugh too often; in 1840, simple and joyous high spirits were hardly admissible when 'learned' music was in question. But it must be understood that if the majority of eighteenth-century minuets—and several types are distinguishable—are put in 'the category of jokes,' it is really impossible to commit a greater error than to include the minuet of the G minor Symphony. In fact, of the whole classical epoch it is perhaps the one minuet whose inspiration springs from the same source as the more scientifically constructed movements of the symphony.

The new and audacious criticism by the romantics, interesting and strong when dealing with contemporary work, was just as ordinary or most often content with commonplaces as soon as the work of the preceding generation came to the surface. Their ideals, no doubt very high, precluded all understanding of the farcical, sometimes 'smart' art with which the eighteenth century was crammed. It was agreed among the 'highbrow' amateurs that Boccherini was no longer bearable; Berlioz emphasizes the '*gaudrioles*' of Haydn; Mozart is pardoned with some difficulty for a few bars of instrumental figuration entrusted to Donna Anna, meditating in her chapel, at the end of *Don Giovanni*. This seems to arise from two distinct causes. Art, generally speaking, tends toward a more severe and grander end; it becomes more individualistic and does not shrink from serving as a constant expression of the personal feelings of the artist, even the most intimate; on the other hand, ignorance of the past, even the near past, clouds everything with so thick a veil that no one can hope to lift it. All the enormous musical richness of Italy, vocal and instrumental, remains a dead letter.

But there was at that time, in the heart of the steppes of central Russia, a man whose ardent love of Mozart's work evoked so profound, living, and a clear vision of this work that he may well be considered the first of the master's real biographers. To his gift of subtle insight were added natural and imaginative qualities of style that allowed him to describe with all the brilliance and fire of his temperament any of Mozart's works, whether operatic, instrumental, or sacred. No one before him had even attempted to span so considerable and diverse a work. Moreover, no book quite like this had ever been devoted to a musician! It is not that of a pedagogue, still less that of an amateur; the analyses it provides of the

great creations of Mozart's genius are almost always
really poetical transformations, but they are backed by
a sufficiently informed musical knowledge to give them
value and solidity. We have already here an example of
sound and trustworthy musicology, and I long to quote
whole pages. But I must limit myself. I shall draw attention to some striking passages dealing with the G minor
Symphony which will give the reader some idea of a
work that is, in my opinion, without precedent, for
until that time no one had had the least idea of a 'musical
biography.'

It was therefore to a Russian nobleman, Alexander
Dimitrievich Ulibichev (1791–1858), that fell the honor
of having attempted the first 'musical' biographical
study of Mozart.[32] In analyzing his principal works in
chronological order he has in fact written something
very like a 'musical life' of the master; the host of needless digressions, it will be realized, is evidence of the
leisure the noble dilettante enjoyed, and it will be understood that all the part treating of musical history and,
in general, his writings on Beethoven's æsthetic are
nowadays entirely in disrepute. But I do not know of
the existence, even today, of many analyses of Mozart's
dramatic works that are comparable with his, as much
from the truly psychological as the musical point of
view; furthermore, no one before him had written so
extensively or brought to bear so much imagination in
commenting on a single quartet or symphony. It would
even be desirable, both out of respect to this direct an-
cestor of the science of musicology and out of admira-

---

[32] *Nouvelle Biographie de Mozart*, followed by a sketch of the
general history of music and *L'Analyse des principales œuvres de
Mozart* (3 volumes), (Moscow: Semen; 1843).

tion for his amazing Mozartian insight, to consider a
reissue of his work, limiting oneself, however, to the
third volume. The author's Slav mysticism enables him
to enter the most secret places of the heart, and to translate into words something that does really give a little
idea of the mysterious beauty of the andante of the G
minor Symphony:

'. . . But what vision glimpsed through the ivory
gates of Elysium, or rather what distant, dim hope has
come to stay this grief, to solace the soul like some divine balm applied to its wounds? *Andante* 6/8 E flat
major, one of those unfathomable works wherein all is
revelation for the feelings and mystery for the mind.
The theme is somewhat vague in its contours, complex
in form, and it is *precisely* from this fact that the movement draws the magic of its effect, and an angelic expression that attains the supernatural. A close inspection
is required to convince oneself that this masterpiece,
varied and rich in figuration as it appears, is built entirely on the first four measures, with in addition another idea, inseparable from the theme but of quite a
different aspect. This is a little figure of thirty-second
notes, grouped in pairs, whose fluttering of wings is
heard mingling with the weightiest syncopations, the
most picturesque harmonic progressions, the most unexpected flights of modulation, the most abstruse thematic "analysis." Add to this a limpid and as it were
prismatic scoring, the same details colored with a multitude of different tints according as they are entrusted
to the bow or human lips; and amid this harmonious
ferment float fragments of song straight from heaven,
as a breath of scent-laden air.' [33]

[33] Ibid., Vol. III, p. 257.

And later, dealing with the transport of passion evident in the finale:

'I doubt if there exists in all music anything more deeply incisive, more cruelly anguished, more violently distracted, more agonizingly passionate than the second half of this finale. And in achieving so exuberant an expression Mozart has employed hardly any means but the main theme, whose motif, at first founded on the intervals of the triad, here utilizes the intervals of the minor ninth and other harmonic acerbities. The theme, too, here splits up in canonic form between the two phalanxes of the orchestra, battling against hostile countersubjects in its furious march, and soon hurled to the ground; then, victor in its turn, you hear it driving pitilessly and relentlessly in a succession of chords which, sharper and sharper, push it to the farthest remove from its primitive tonality; and all this continues for 80 measures. From what incident of his inner life, what paroxysm of the heart, has Mozart drawn this frenzied yet classic inspiration? How has this abundance of passion sprung from such an abundance of skill!' [34] The Russian critic, in the lines following, sums up the general impression made on him by the G minor Symphony; his refined appreciation, in fact, corroborates that of the first hearers of the masterpiece:

'The G minor Symphony, like the quintet in the same key, expresses the disturbance of passion, the longing and regret of an unhappy love, but it expresses them with the difference that here we have a plaint concentrated, in the depths of his own soul, or at most suffered vicariously through the sympathy of a friend, on a grief without reserve and without bounds, bursting in the

[34] Ibid., pp. 259–60.

face of the whole world, which it would fill with its lamentations.' [35]

On almost every page of the book similar appraisals are to be found; Berlioz apart, music had never, I believe, been previously spoken of in like terms. The Russian critic wrote these lines about the year 1841: who knows? perhaps we see in him the Sainte-Beuve of musical criticism, with his enthusiasms and his prejudices; in any case, we see in him a man not content with anecdotes more or less diverting, but one who often speaks of music with the finest discrimination, one who goes to the root of the matter and boldly plunges into the realm of psychology. He is at home there with the easy elegance of the diplomat who has learned to know his fellow men; in artistic matters he gives judgment with a clear vision free from all pedantry. But for any musical work dating after about 1815 or 1820 one feels that his sensitivity is dulled and his judgment warped. For bear in mind that he was born in 1791, the very year of Mozart's death! Who then of his generation would have grasped the significance of Beethoven's last works, or of the first flowerings of romanticism? On the other hand, those who did feel the transcendence of the work of the later Beethoven relegated all Mozart's instrumental work, *ipso facto*, to the second class. The main point is that no one had as yet (that is, before 1841) surveyed this work with so acute and comprehensive a glance.

Unhappily, the book was not able to exorcize a sort of decline, or at least a slackening off in the interest aroused by Mozart's instrumental music in the second half of the nineteenth century. In contrast to this his dramatic works continued to have a following, and at

[35] Ibid., p. 255.

every production of one or another of his operas their
success had been maintained, or even heightened. And
that up to the moment when, the Wagnerian movement
absorbing everything, Mozart's vocal and symphonic
work had disappeared almost completely below the musical horizon. Wagnerism admitted scarcely anything
but the Beethoven of the last quartets, the Mass in D,
and the Choral Symphony.

And here we must note the most curious phenomenon of all. For, if we have established the almost complete disappearance of Mozart's symphonic works from
the programs of the great concerts of the Wagner period, and even if a certain disdain for his work in general is in evidence at this time, it is all the more surprising to learn that the most undoubtedly illustrious of all
the Wagnerians—Richard Wagner himself—has revealed himself as the most ardent and comprehensive
protagonist of Mozart's three great symphonies. The
perusal of Volume IX of his writings came as a surprise
and a revelation to us. What I have said above of his
preoccupations relative to the interpretation of Mozart,
and especially of the E flat Symphony, of which he
demonstrates the artistic sense and importance equally
with regard to the first movement and the finale, has already thrown a sufficient light on his Mozartian feeling.[36]

When he had the opportunity of hearing the G minor
Symphony at the famous concerts at the Odeon in Munich, the detailed description of the andante (from
which he quotes three passages) and the ironic criticism
he gives of this performance enable one to see the extent
of his admiration, and how much he felt the interpreta-

[36] Wagner, op. cit.

tion of a great masterpiece (victim of an already long-standing tradition) left to be desired. The passage should be quoted in its entirety:

'. . . I was present at the performance of the G minor Symphony of Mozart. The manner in which the *Andante* of the symphony was played, and the effect it produced was altogether inconceivable. Who has not, in his youth, admired this beautiful piece, and tried to realise it in his own way? In what way? No matter. If the marks of expression are scanty, the wonderful composition arouses one's feelings; and fancy supplies the means to read it in accordance with such feelings. It seems as if Mozart had expected something of the kind, for he has given but few and meagre indications of the expressions. So we felt free to indulge ourselves in the delicately increasing swing of the quavers, with the moon-like rise of the violins; the notes of which we believed to sound softly legato:

*98

the tenderly whispering:

*99

touched us as with wings of angels, and before the solemn admonitions and questionings of:

*100

(which, however, we heard in a finely sustained *crescendo*) we imagined ourselves led to a blissful evanescence, which came upon us with the final bars. Fancies of this sort, however, were not permitted during the strictly classical performance under the veteran Kapellmeister, at the Munich Odeon: the proceedings, there, were carried on with a degree of solemnity enough to make one's flesh creep with a sensation akin to a foretaste of eternal perdition.

'The lightly floating *Andante* was converted into a ponderous *Largo;* not the hundredth part of the weight of a single quaver was spared us; stiff and ghastly, like a bronze pigtail, the *battuta* of the *Andante* was swung over our heads; even the feathers of the angels' wings were turned into corkscrew curls—rigid, like those of the Seven Years' War. Already, I felt myself placed under the staff of a Prussian recruiting officer, A.D. 1740, and longed to be bought off—but! who can guess my terror, when the veteran turned back the pages, and recommenced his *Largo-Andante* merely to do 'Classical' justice to the two little dots before the double bar in the score! I looked about me for help and succour—and beheld another wondrous thing: the audience listened patiently, quite convinced that everything was in the best possible order, and that they were having a true Mozartian 'feast for the ears' in all innocence and safety. This being so, I acquiesced and bowed my head in silence.' [37]

Certainly, nothing comparable has been written on Mozart since Ulibichev. No commentary by his accredited biographers has this ring: I cannot be too as-

[37] Richard Wagner: *The Art of Conducting* (Dannreuther's translation, pp. 62 ff.).

tonished for my own part, for Wyzewa and I had been struck, Wyzewa first, by evident quasi-Wagnerian kinship spread over different periods of Mozart's career. But we would not have dared to point them out in so pungent a fashion; under the pretext of teaching the art of conducting, or simply proffering advice, Wagner unveils all his sensitivity and understanding in the presence of masterpieces usually considered as the farthest removed from his own art and thought. Besides, his insistence on the degree of error and incomprehension that prevails over the question of the interpretation of Mozart's instrumental works shows how profound was his response and what artistic value he attributes to them. It was in great measure for the maintenance of their cult and the revival of their spirit that he solicited from his sovereign the favor of being allowed to create a new school of music in Germany. But he always put Mozart's vocal or theatrical work first, and it is probable that of the instrumental music he knew only the last three symphonies. However that may be, these occupy a prominent place in his thoughts and artistic preoccupations.

Today it can be stated without exaggeration that in publishing the fifth edition of Otto Jahn's celebrated *Life of Mozart*, Herr Hermann Abert has almost supplanted the work of his predecessor.[38] His work constitutes one of the finest monuments erected to the glory of Mozart's genius; he illumines all its aspects without forcing all Mozart's output, willy-nilly, into the framework of a pre-established æsthetic; we feel so much, on reading Abert's two volumes, what was the univer-

[38] Hermann Abert: *W. A. Mozart* (2 volumes) (Leipzig: Breitkopf & Härtel; 1921).

sality of Mozart's genius that this demonstration becomes a veritable revelation. It can be said of these two
volumes that they complete the overthrow of nearly
all that the criticism of the romantic period would ad-
mit on the subject of Mozart, not merely as to the theatrical work, but equally concerning the instrumental
output and the sacred music. It is a Mozart completely
stripped of the costume in which Otto Jahn had clothed
him according to the fashions of the 1860's. From now
on, this fifth edition is an entirely new book with little
connection with the work of its precursor; everything
in the latter that was merely conventional has become
transformed into significance. For my part, the author
has opened up horizons so new and vast that I can still
hardly visualize the goal further research will attain.
Those who believe the subject of Mozart to be exhausted
are given the lie by Abert's two volumes. Equally in the
field of human psychology [39] as in that of æsthetic and
documentary study, these two volumes of German
musicology are an inducement to delve into everything,
even what is apparently frivolous.

The analysis of the great symphonies proves to what
a slender degree of understanding we were until then
accustomed with regard to these masterpieces—with the
exception, I must add immediately, of those veritable
and penetrating æsthetical and musicological analyses of
Alexander Ulibichev, and Richard Wagner's confes-
sions. For the first time Abert shows us the direct kinship between the great introduction to the E flat Symphony and the dramatic preface to *Don Giovanni;* in
stressing the already profoundly romantic character of

[39] See particularly the remarkable chapter entitled: "Mozart's
Personality," Vol. II, p. 1.

this symphony he thus prepares us for the description
of another drama, quite as forceful though more concise, which is none other than the G minor Symphony:
the analytical pictures he draws of this, and of Mozart's
symphonic apotheosis (the C major Symphony, the
'Jupiter'), are real interpretations, out of which the
author derives a new philosophy, which he elucidates
with a rare felicity of expression. From the examination
of the texts springs at once their 'intellectual' intepreta-
tion, and we thus see revealed what is still almost unsuspected: namely, the profound meaning of the orchestral masterpiece. Here is surely the most profound
commentary to which the instrumental work of Mozart
in its final stages has given rise.

Wyzewa and I had already established that Mozart's
last three symphonies, nearly contemporaneous with
Don Giovanni, marked the apex of his romantic career:
reading the various commentaries inspired by one or
other of them affords some confirmation of this fact.
What has been written with pen of flame would naturally excite the most glowing and ardent description;
and nowhere are there to be found any appreciations
comparable with those that *Don Giovanni* and the G
minor Symphony have inspired. For the latter, we have
been able to follow the crescendo of admiration extended to it by critics since its first performances in
France and Germany, until the time of the publications
of Ulibichev (1843), Otto Jahn (1856), Richard Wagner (1865–9), and Abert (1921). Between these last two
works criticism recognized with great difficulty the passionate character of the symphony; it insisted, as indeed
for every work dating from the eighteenth century, on
its graceful movement, or simply on its melancholy. For

us the G minor Symphony, with a more reduced orchestra than in Mozart's other great symphonic compositions, translates the inner unrest of a mind that has always chosen this key for the expression of feelings of
ardent and troubled melancholy, infinitely impassioned.

Symphony in C Major (the 'Jupiter') [40]

Completed August 10, 1788

The orchestra includes, besides the string quartet
(where cellos are quite distinct from the double basses),
one flute, two oboes, two bassoons, two horns (in C),
two trumpets (in C), and timpani (C, G).

*101—K.551.

The first part of the movement (before the double
bar line) can be divided into five sections, separated
from one another sometimes by a pedal point, or by
pauses twice lasting three beats of a bar and once, to
make the contrast even more marked, a whole bar. From
these five portions we get an impression of vital force
that often enhances the martial, heroic character which
the movement owes to the march rhythm of the wind
instruments.

The work opens with a rough triplet figure, a sort of
'appel heroïque' to be found in many a symphony or

[40] The person responsible for this nickname, dating certainly
from after the death of Mozart, is unknown.

overture, here intensified by the unison of strings and
wind. This principle of masculine affirmation is at once
succeeded by a sort of plaintive questioning, clearly
standing for the expressive, feminine principle, as distinct from the dominating element stated at the beginning of the movement. Then, a new opposition between
this dominating force stated once more, now in the
dominant, and the same response, a degree higher and
thus rendered even more expressive. The latter is
quickly cut short by an orchestral *tutti*, with the whole
of the wind outlining a solemn but lively march, punctuated by big chords on the first violins. Between these
emphatic chords the second violins and violas are heard
with a descending flourish seemingly corresponding to
the rising triplets of the opening. All this constitutes a
ritornello of great dignity, proclaiming a sort of triumph
closely akin to that Mozart will later write to open his
Clemenza di Tito. What I have called the first section,
the foundation stone of the building, closes with a long
pedal point ending with the whole orchestra in unison,
on the dominant. So behold this cornerstone laid before
us with the most irresistible vigor and clearness, in the
full, frank light of C major.

But now a tiny cloud appears in the sky. The opening
theme is repeated, but piano, as it were softened and
overcome by a new figure (flute and oboe), which
modifies and refines its first roughness; the response,
which seemed just now restrained and almost stifled, is
extended:

*102

diversified by the dramatic inflections so peculiar to
Mozart, and is to play an essential role in this second
section of the movement. In fact, from the moment
when the first measure of Ex.101 has re-echoed, forte,
in the dominant, this melodic response becomes so warm
and intense that its rhythm dominates the orchestra and
its importance becomes preponderating in all the rest of
the movement; but despite its melodic character and
ardent expression, the horns and trumpets maintain the
march rhythm, accentuated, and reproduce in a slightly
abridged form the martial ritornello that formerly ended
on the dominant, over a pedal point, and which is here
brusquely interrupted by a chord of the dominant of G.
After three beats' rest the true second subject of the
movement emerges in the first violins:

*103

to which the basses will later reply with a sort of evoca-
tive echo of the above-mentioned melodic response
(measure 71); in the second exposition of this subject
the first violins are joined by the bassoon, and later by
the flute, without in the least detracting from its airy
suppleness. Its length is such that by itself it fills the
whole of this third section; and that shows to what extent Mozart delighted in dialogues between the mem-
bers of the quartet during this episode, which exceeds
in length all the second subjects of his symphonies.

But the heroic atmosphere of the symphony cannot

allow this second subject to be established too firmly, as
its delightful suppleness runs the risk of modifying the
general character of the movement. So everything is cut
short abruptly; there is a whole measure's rest, then the
outburst, forte, in the minor:

*104

leading very quickly to a ritornello demonstrating anew
the force of that melodic response which simultaneously
plays a role both expressive and rhythmic, a role whose
importance in the movement is certainly as great as that
of the separate subjects constituting it. In it, in fact,
there lies an intrinsic power that spreads throughout
the whole movement, with the exception, however, of
the development.

Then, after a new bar on an unexpected figure on the
dominant of G major, a new figure emerges in this key,
light in character, straight out of *opera buffa:* [41]

*105

Seeing this bubbling up in its carefree buoyancy, one
would never guess that from it, or more exactly from its

[41] It had appeared already in an air written by Mozart in May
1788, for Albertarelli, to the words: "*Voi siete un po tondo, mio
caro Pompeo, l'usanze del mondo andate a studiar.*"

immediate sequence, would spring all the first part of
that enormous development, one of Mozart's most spacious and powerful! This fifth section of the movement
demonstrates its unwonted breadth; it surpasses the
usual limits of the master's great symphonies, and brings
to the general gravity of the work a playful note from
which Mozart can draw more science than from a theme
more inherently 'scholastic.' Finally, the first part of the
movement concludes with a ritornello in which, at the
very end, the figure or roulade in descending thirty-
second notes that has already intruded in the first two
sections of the movement takes a prominent part.

The development opens with two measures of flutes,
oboes, and bassoons in unison, taking us quietly and almost playfully into the dark key of E-flat major. With
the same bass accompaniment and the same viola pizzicato, but this time in E flat, we are reintroduced to the
charming and unexpected theme that had served as a
conclusion to the first part (Ex.105). It is a curious
thing, as I have already remarked, that the most scholarly part of the work has been drawn from this theme,
or rather from its last measure, which is at once repeated by oboes and bassoons accompanied by the
basses pizzicato. This measure is immediately interchanged between violins and basses while the march
rhythm that we have noticed earlier reappears in the
wind; after six measures the counterpoint becomes
more closely knit, the two groups are thrown against
each other in the same measure, beneath sustained
chords in the wind, until the basses seize the subject and
exhaust its 'potential'; they conduct it to the point
where it serves only as a transition leading back to the
first subject, after two measures of unaccompanied

woodwind have brought us to rest on the dominant of
A minor:

*106

All this is but a dry analysis; but how can one give any
idea whatever of the vitality that emerges, the most
symphonically in the world, from all this development?
Never has the term *development* been used in a more
correct and inspired sense than here: while the woodwinds are outlining lofty and joyous rhythms, while the
strings exchange among themselves that little figure derived from the simple final cadence of the third and last
subject of the movement, and while all this is combined
by an intrinsic force capable of unifying all and still
ruling, behold the miracle by which Mozart, at grips
with the most diverse elements of symphony, chamber
music, or operatic finale, becomes the supreme master
sporting divinely with these elements.

But the development is not finished, and, as it were, a
second one now commences: for the size of this last
symphony is going to surpass all expectation! Nearly
seven pages of the Eulenburg miniature score are filled
by the development of the first movement, which has a
total length of twenty-nine pages. So after a few measures, wherein we see the final expiry of the little figure
that has been the mainspring of all the development so
far, in passing from the dominant of A minor to the key
of F major, we shall witness a new and powerful development, opening with a return to the principal subject in F—a circumstance at once directing our minds

to a procedure especially dear to Josef Haydn and
which has been designated by the term *false recapitulation*. We have here, indeed, just such a false recapitulation; this sly and unexpected return of the principal
theme, piano, in improvisatory fashion, and at first seemingly intent on passing unperceived, becomes firmly established in the orchestra; each repetition takes it a degree higher in the scale, with constant support from the
chromaticisms of the woodwind; on its first appearance,
in F, it is still followed by its melodic response, but from
the second appearance onwards this has vanished.
Events move rapidly, and the conflict threatens. It
breaks out on a chord of A minor; then, over a bass descending semitone by semitone, with syncopated chords
in the woodwind, a violent struggle flares up between
the triplet figure with which the movement began and
that launched by the second violins and violas under the
martial calls of the wind. These two contrary figures,
the one ascending, the other descending, are given at
first to the violins, who hurl and hustle them through
the roughest tonalities, until the basses seize on the second and bring it to a halt on the dominant. Next, the
cadence of the third subject, from which all the first
development had sprung, reappears in the first violins
and in the space of eight measures leads to the recapitulation. But this cadence, so fertile in unforeseen counter-
points, is again to give rise in this space to a masterly
stroke, allotted to the woodwind alone; and it is an unalloyed pleasure to see, or hear, the oboes and bassoons
yielding to new ideas, such as the great working-out of
this unique figure in the first development had not allowed us to foresee. Such is the magnificent scaffolding:
when at first the master magician showed us the two or

three poor little fragments that were to be used in constructing it and raising it up in all its grandeur, we certainly could not have deduced the technical and æsthetic result obtained by Mozart—a power uniquely musical wherein genius itself is forgotten.

In the great works of Mozart the repercussion exercised by similar developments on the subsequent course of the movement is so considerable that, even where the recapitulation is identical with the opening, its component elements are seen to be as it were transfigured: there is an occult and inexpressible force, a sort of surging of the elements stirred by the powerful, all-commanding helm. And that is the impression we get of this recapitulation; the only changes appear in the second statement of the theme after the long pedal point on the dominant. The second statement this time is in the minor, and the melodic response gives rise to some counterpoint that yields an elevated moment of six measures' duration.

*107

By their reappearance all the elements of the movement acquire that character of definitive significance that a single exposition could not confer on them, and it is perhaps in this fact that we can find rational justification for the repetition of all the elements of a movement, so often criticized by the non-musical. There remains nothing now but the conclusion. Mozart simply adds a few measures in which resounds a fanfare that winds up the first movement of the 'Jupiter' in a mood of joyous steadfastness.

*108

The theme is stated by the first violins *con sordini;* it is joined in the lower octave by the seconds, then accompanied by them and the violas, both muted. Its length (ten measures) is as remarkable as its expression. It can be looked upon as formed of two phrases; the second, beginning at the seventh measure, is a song of warm and expansive tenderness, so spontaneous that it becomes almost an outburst of this feeling, as if the heart could no longer contain it. The sentence finishes and, having concluded in the tonic, the melody then passes to the violas and basses (cellos and double basses), with repeated chords on horns and bassoons in support; almost at once the violins reply to this melody with a figure in thirty-second notes, an offshoot of the theme itself, leading by a beautiful descending curve to the dominant, and the second subject.

The latter by successive stages reaches its culmination at the end of its seventh measure; it begins in the minor, and immediately syncopations and sighs throw us into an atmosphere of trouble and grief, and that, too, most 'modern' in feeling; the chords of the ninth and the audacious modulations combine to create an impression very near to that of many Wagnerian fragments; but with the transience of a cloud melting before the rays of the sun—and, we might add, with something of the same nature—the third subject appears in the first violins accompanied by embroidery in the seconds and with the basses in contrary motion. This is a rising phrase, like the preceding one, floating in a limitless ether; it is answered by a figure in sextuplets destined to play an important part in the remainder of this andante, a figure whose varied and charming curves have a melancholy tinge, probably due to the impression left by the second subject. It is necessary to insist on the length of these subjects, particularly the last, which is followed by a ritornello in the form of a dialogue between wind and strings; this over, the first violins, still preserving the sextuplet motion, help us over the double bar, alone and unaided, in the most original fashion.

This unexpected transition has something of the air of a recitative. But it has gone scarcely four measures before the winds have already repeated the second subject, perhaps even more plaintive than on its first presentation. From D minor we pass to E-flat minor, and arrive at the recapitulation by means of a dialogue between wind and strings fashioned out of a fragment of the preceding sextuplets, flowing in incessant chromaticisms.

But what changes in this recapitulation! Scarcely has the first measure of the theme sounded in the first violins, when the slurred thirty-second-note figure that answered the initial theme in the first part of the andante appears in the basses; by its very nature this vast flowing figure so belongs to the violins that they now seize it afresh; it is interrupted, however, to allow the first measure of the theme to resound in the basses, in B flat. Then,

forte, the torrent of thirty-second notes sweeps irresistibly from under the bows, with *'appels héroïques'* from
the wind: the culminating-point is reached in a veritable
fracas over the dominant; a fortissimo blazes out, with
the thirty-second notes in the basses, the woodwind and
horns hammering out their rhythm on the chord of C
major and the violins slashing great chords across three
strings. Then, with no transition, a brief echo of the second subject is heard, as it were a sob quickly stifled; and
the third subject reappears complete with its expressive
continuation suffused with an Elysian calm and heightened by new wonders in the treatment of the wind. The
dialogue noticed above is reproduced, leading to one of
the most beautiful codas Mozart has ever conceived.

The first measure of the theme is sung, as at first, by
the first violins; but in place of the second the thirty-
second-note figure appears, piano, on the flute and
bassoon in octaves. The second half of the theme, so
intensely expressive, which had been omitted in the recapitulation, is here reproduced in its entirety, in all its
ravishing simplicity; and of the long figure in sextuplets
there remain only the last two measures of the movement, a sort of far-off, poetic echo, expiring in a pianissimo not unlike the ending of the slow movement of the
G minor Symphony.[42]

*109

Menuetto. Allegretto

---

[42] This fine ending replaces another, shorter one. See Abert,
op. cit., Vol. II, p. 133.

This minuet is assuredly one of the most original Mozart ever wrote for symphony orchestra. It should be noted that it comprises but a single subject and constitutes a perfect little sonata-form movement, with development and recapitulation. The same could be said of other minuets; but this one seems to form an even more homogeneous whole.

With its chromaticisms, it offers us at the outset a language whose sensuality is interrupted, nine measures after the double bar line, only to allow the wind instruments to ring out, unaccompanied by strings: chromaticisms, symphonic writing of the richest kind, the use of the wind, all put us in mind of Wagner; and the likeness becomes even more obvious when, a few measures before the end, the wind, entirely unaccompanied, interlace their chromatically descending lines! This passage for unaccompanied wind does in fact reproduce the procedure Mozart employs in the corresponding place in the minuet of the G minor Symphony, but how much developed and amplified here! The outstandingly 'modern' character of this minuet is affirmed by the intensive use of counterpoint, almost presaging the role this will play in the ensuing finale. The trio, likewise, seems to herald the near approach of the famous finale; the first notes of the latter are, in fact, already outlined in the first-violin part, immediately after the double bar.

This anticipation is worthy of remark, for the first notes of the succeeding finale must have assumed a definite significance in Mozart's work. They are in fact to be found scattered among several works of different character—Mass, symphony, sonata for violin and piano —but it is in the coming finale that they receive their definite and final consecration.

*110

This famous movement, considered, and with justification, perhaps the veritable symphonic testament of
Mozart, is not a fugue, as has so often been stated. It is a
complex ensemble, very difficult to classify in pre-
established forms, in which counterpoint plays a preponderant role destined to reveal Mozart as complete
master of his resources. But it is first and foremost a
movement in *sonata form*, with repeat bars, development, and varied recapitulation, followed by a grand
coda.

This preponderating use of *fugato* in a symphonic
finale was not unprecedented. The Austrian instrumental school has examples to offer that have become known
only recently: probably under the influence of the old
contrapuntist Fux, whose not inconsiderable reaction is
felt up to the time of Beethoven, such masters as Georg
Matthias Monn, Dittersdorf, Michael Haydn (a first-
hand exemplar for Mozart) practiced the *fugato* finale
form in their symphonies, without, of course, even re-
motely approaching the effect that Mozart here obtained. What is worthy of note here is the coexistence
of the scholastic element in a quartet or symphony finale
side by side with other themes of a less severe nature,
even popular or trifling; the best example of this genre

is the finale of the first of the six quartets dedicated to Josef Haydn. Nevertheless here the quality of the themes does not present such an alloy, and their combination does not offer so striking a contrast: the general bearing of the symphony, which, one feels, Mozart has thoroughly understood, does not allow of such license in the choice of material. And that the very diverse and individual themes forming the substance of the present finale should cohere into such admirable unity is not the least astonishing merit of this gigantic musical peroration.

It is possible to distinguish three gigantic fragments composing in reality the first portion of the movement. In the first of these the themes (a) and (b) figure; the first actually comprising two halves, one formed of the four-note motif, familiar since, as I have remarked, it forms a favorite group used by Mozart in many a vocal and instrumental work, while the other plays only a brilliant and homophonic role and will be used in the ritornello and at the end of the coda.

The movement opens, piano, with an astonishingly simple melodic phrase, stated by the first violins to an accompaniment of slurred eighth notes in the seconds. The whole orchestra is at once brought into play for the counter-statement; the melody continues to be entrusted to the violins, but staccato, while in the treble the wind is busy with a severe motif, in suspensions, and in the bass the lower strings trace roulades of three or four sixteenth notes, clearly derived from the four sixteenth notes that give a sort of surge to the refrain. The first subject being now ended in the tonic, a new idea (b), clear and vigorous, arises. It is easy to see that it will lend itself to numerous combinations; it engenders

and demands contrapuntal treatment. But one could
scarcely suspect its hidden force of attraction in this regard. Here it is as it is first heard:

*111

Over a bass moving by contrary motion it climbs a third
higher, presently to reappear in the wittiest and most
unexpected fashion, divested of all its weighty and ma-
jestic contrapuntal character, piped by a solo flute as a
response to the true cantabile subject of the movement,
in the third section of the finale (Ex.113). A brilliant
ritornello, quite homophonic, brings us to rest on the
dominant.

The second period opens with the initial whole notes,
piano, attacked first by the second violins, next by the
firsts, then the violas, and lastly by the basses; veritable
fugal entries, following one another at intervals of three
and four measures. Strictly limited to the string quartet
at first, this dominating theme is then repeated in octaves by the upper parts (violins, flutes, and oboes),
with a new sequel:

*112

giving rise in its turn to imitations between violins and
basses, supported by the whole of the wind; and as this
section is to be devoted wholly to polyphony, it is not
surprising to find motif (b) reappearing here, as a *co-
detta*, generating imitations at half a measure's distance.
This contraction does not really allow sufficient time for
the imitations to be clearly heard in so quick a movement; we would go so far as to say its character here
becomes a trifle flurried.

We now have the cantabile subject of the movement:

*113

which opens the third section in G major. Stated piano
by the first violins to an eighth-note accompaniment in
the seconds, exactly like the first subject, it is succeeded
by the witty response derived from theme (b), already
noted above (page 169). By its very Mozartian grace, its
delicate playfulness, it seems to exclude the severity and
roughness of counterpoint. But no such thing: Mozart
here is as insistent as possible, and seems bent on demonstrating to future generations the resources of the old
language, its richness and persuasive force. I am fully in
agreement with Abert, who does not hesitate to recog-

nize in the composer of *Don Giovanni* the last repre-
sentative of the old school of contrapuntists, those for
whom counterpoint was neither an effort nor a display
of learning, but a mode of expression, a language that
Mozart revived, all the resources of which he was able
to adapt to the needs of modern thought.

His way of combining this melodious subject with
the sequel to the first subject quoted in Ex.112 and
motif (b) (Ex.111) is as dexterous as it is audacious. It
is a dialogue in which counterpoint becomes mocking
and carefree. First, flutes and bassoons, in imitation, exchange Ex.112 between them to the accompaniment of
a running violin figure; we next behold the subject that
had seemed uniquely melodic (Ex.113) transformed
into a fugal entry, retaining no more than its first three
half notes and, shedding its singing character, acquiring
an unforeseen vigor and becoming clearly scholastic:

It is interchanged between the first violins and the
basses, while the second violins and the violas are themselves engaged in a spirited duel in eighth notes. But
Mozart is about to show us that it is not only the three
opening notes of Ex.113 that are capable of becoming
very respectable fugal entries, but the entire theme. And
now, the battle being first joined by the strings, with
the woodwind admitting in the first place only the three
half notes mentioned above, feeling runs so high that

they fling themselves bravely into the melee; and so powerful is the surge of all this that what I have called the refrain of the initial subject blazes up with a brilliance so vivid that, suddenly, all counterpoint ceases and the homophony of the refrain gains the mastery. But this simple refrain, growing in force and extent, is quickly seized by the basses, modulates, and leads to some brusque imitations of (b) which will later resolve into a ritornello destined to close the first part in the key of the dominant. Our description would seem to indicate a cadence, forte, in a brilliant style; this astonishing movement yields on the contrary the surprise of ending with a short coda through which flits motif (b), first like a farewell in the storm, first presented hastily on the oboe, and repeated by the bassoon.

After this contest, of which words are powerless to convey its variety and spirit, its verve and dominating energy, what could possibly be the development now about to commence? What development can follow the two developments already completed?

It opens after the double bar with the return of the principal subject, like all regularly constructed sonata-form movements. It modulates at once to C minor; the wind replies, piano, with motif (b), on oboe and bassoon; and these first three measures of the second part are sufficient, solely by means of modulation, to throw a mysterious veil over the first subject:

*115

When the latter reappears over the dominant of A minor, the same response is introduced anew, but inverted, and the bitter conflict that had previously been unleashed in the course of the second section is at once renewed. Here, at half a measure's distance, imitations between basses, violins, and wind are built up once more; I have previously remarked on their compression and speed, motif (b) opening with a dotted quarter note followed by an eighth note, bursting so promptly in the various instrumental groups that their successive discharges have insufficient time to be clearly heard by the listener. I have mentioned how (b) was developed in both ascending and descending fashion; when it occurs in ascending form, giving rise to a like combat in a clash of imitations, Mozart finds means of intercalating the first subject between each new attack, modulating fifth upon fifth, and stated by wind alone. Here is the layout, quasi-Tristanesque in style:

*116

The incessant and aggressive response (b), which has become a forceful and leading theme, continues in the strings until, on the dominant of E minor and sounding in unison, the master's genius requires six measures only in which to get back to the principal subject in the original key. The passage is worth quoting:

*117

This is a powerful abridgment. The recapitulation
will provide another, not less energetic. The principal
subject is stated, as at first, by the first violins, accompanied in the same fashion by the slurred eighth notes
in the seconds; but the woodwinds join in rather earlier,
before the energetic counter-statement, staccato, on the
violins; the basses again roll out their figure, rising and
falling like the waves of the ocean. Not content with
the three or four measures of the exposition, they here
extend through twenty measures, and enter many harmonic domains; their impact has the effect of deepening
considerably all this recapitulation and of swelling the
expressive content of the first subject.

Motif (b), which sounded in heroic fashion on its
first statement, will be seen to be very much reduced in
the recapitulation; the imitations of Ex.112 are renewed
between the basses and the first violins, and the shocks
imparted to motif (b) by imitations in stretti are reduced to five measures—not surprising since (b) had
borne by itself practically all the burden of the portion
following the double bar; that is to say, all that takes the
place of the normal development in a sonata-form movement.

And now, this time, all the fugued passage on (a)
forming the opening of the second section has entirely
vanished; the cantabile subject returns, and the entire
third section is reproduced with no alterations save some

changes in the disposition of the instrumental parts. My
observations on the subject of this third section are
therefore applicable anew here; but I must add that the
return of the theme to the tonic and the repetition of
the final refrain or ritornello give to the whole an air as
of apotheosis; as for the section preceding the double
bars, the approach of these provides us again with the
surprise of a premature and softened ending. For here
we find new repeat marks, separating the final coda
clearly from all that has gone before.

We now have arrived at the pathetic moment when
Mozart sums the whole thing up by way of conclusion.
He finds means to present the component themes of the
movement in a new light, inverting the first (a) and su-
perposing the others on it. We might with justice have
supposed that Mozart, before writing this coda (which
he could have treated as a simple final stretto), had
drawn from these themes all they were capable of in
point of musical force, of vital energy. But the coda
shows us that, without combining them in a regular
fugue, but giving free rein to the contrapuntal force
they conceal, they can still reveal unknown resources
and, blending with each other, finally blaze out in a
dazzling display of tonal pyrotechnics.

All here is strictly thematic. After having renewed,
forte, the imitations on motif (b) immediately after the
double bar, brusquely attacked by the whole orchestra
on the seventh chord in the key of F major, we have the
initial motif, completely transformed, and assuming an
expression of distant melancholy; despite all our previ-
sion, the handling of these four notes did not seem to
hold the promise of such a result! But the possibilities of
genius are limitless, and there is something of magic in

this power of renewing the color and expression of a given theme:

*118

then, suddenly, the melodic motif (Ex.113) emerges in the violas, likewise transformed by a brusque fugal attack, while the first subject is stated by basses, bassoons, and horns. Then the sequel (Ex.112), and another figure, first heard on the oboe immediately after the melodic subject in the third section of the movement (measure 76), join in the combat. Very soon afterwards all the combatant forces find themselves in the struggle, in a page wherein the maximum of intrinsic power of the different themes, the climax of their vital energy, their cohesion, is attained by the master with the most complete success. Now that the great encounter has been joined their *élan* becomes clearer; these elements, immeasurably ennobled by battle, are merged and resolved in a return of the refrain that followed the first subject. Once again (b) re-echoes in unison, and Mozart marks the conclusion with a fanfare, heroic and brief.

Despite the enormous musical weightiness of this symphonic testament of Mozart it can scarcely be affirmed that the 'Jupiter' Symphony received the unanimous approval or the almost immediate acclamation of the E flat and G minor symphonies; perhaps the vast plan of the work and especially the complexity of the finale perplexed its first hearers. The fact is that before this masterly *chef-d'œuvre* criticism itself was also dumbfounded. Had not Mozart here pushed his audacities beyond permissible bounds? Again, did he not rely too much on the skill of the performers? A multitude of petty reasons cropped up, as usual in the presence of a still unknown great work. For, with not the slightest risk of self-deception, we can say that nothing so great and important had arisen before that which dawned on August 10, 1788; neither in the orchestra nor in any chamber-music center had a comparable work been heard. And now behold Mozart with his bold felicity, for what reason we know not, raising up this brilliant edifice and crowning it with a vast instrumental 'chorus' that saw the older music, suddenly revived, united with the new to salute the future! With a sovereign grace, eloquence, and force, the master in his thirty-second year gathers up all the elements his most glorious predecessors have used and reveals to us all that music has achieved up to his time, and what it will do nearly a hundred years later. That such a work should have proved too difficult for some hearers need not surprise us. If, as I have said, this brilliant edifice has apparently been in shadow, fringed by the dark clouds of the romantic period, today it appears even more radiant, elegant and proud perhaps than in the past. It is raised up in all its C major brightness to the open sky.

In our delving into past criticisms I have already remarked on a notice almost certainly concerned with the 'Jupiter' (see page 108). In the following article from the pen of the composer Michel Bourges, who replaced Hector Berlioz on the *Gazette musicale*, dated March 5, 1843, the lack of understanding and appreciation of the

most remarkable work of the preceding generation is
borne upon us in the clearest fashion:

'Symphony in C, by Mozart

'In this, despite its elegance, its charm of detail, and
despite the enormous facility of the writer, we find too
many out-of-date formulas, too many needless commonplaces, too much aimless and ineffective development, too many laborious technical procedures, especially in the finale. The skill of the performers can
doubtless fascinate and create illusions, but it could not
prevent the adagio from being diffuse and dragging, nor
the last movement from being cold and meaningless, despite its admirable construction—a perfect academic
model.'

In the following year Stephen Heller, in the same
journal, praises the andante and the finale, but regards
this finale as being 'insolently fugal' (February 1844).

The means of expression chosen by Mozart is, in fact,
no longer understood. From the moment fugue appears
on the scene, it is argued, he sheds his soul. And we are
both surprised and pleased to have been able to quote a
French critic of some thirty years earlier, much nearer
to grasping the fundamental musical meaning of this
masterpiece.

It is true that Wagner, about 1830 or 1831, took it as a
direct model in composing his one and only symphony.
'After several other works I set to work on a symphony;
to my prototype Beethoven was added Mozart, especially his great C major Symphony.' [43] But we shall have
occasion to return again to the composer of *Tristan*,

[43] Wagner: *Autobiographische Skizze* (*Autobiographical
Sketches*).

who, taking the 'Jupiter' Symphony as a pattern when he ventured into the realm of the symphony at the outset of his career, remained faithful to Mozart's great work, and discussed it several times in his advice to conductors (1869).

To return to Ulibichev, who concludes his study [44] of Mozart's symphonies with something resembling a musical ode—an expression he himself uses to qualify the C major Symphony:

'One might say that the Symphony in C was commanded and written to celebrate some mighty event in the world's history, a victory of the human mind forever memorable and blessed, accomplished in humanity's own interests. The resounding splendor of the orchestra bursting forth in all its power at the ninth measure establishes beyond all doubt the attitude of triumphant rejoicing as the fundamental character of the work; but the theme preceding this victorious outburst is a double one: it is composed of a species of fanfare, succeeded by a little interrogatory phrase, in slurred notes. The latter is the main motif, the fecund theme that by its developments imprints a unique stamp of spirituality to the great jubilation of the allegro, appealing to the mind as a continued aspiration toward some intellectual summit the lyric poet burns to attain, but can only achieve toward the very end of the ode. Nothing is more magnificent and solemn than the amplifications, transformations, and analyses of these two thematic fragments. The one sounds and resounds like some forest cascade, repeated in several keys by the mountain echoes; the other figure, ever pursuing under diverse forms the goal to which

[44] Ulibichev: *Nouvelle Biographie de Mozart,* Vol. III, pp. 260 ff.

it aspires, now plunges into the bass or floats above in the melody, now concentrated in a vigorous unison, mounting, mounting, it forces a passage between pedal points in the extreme parts of the score, reinforced by a prolonged play of trumpets. An inexpressible, sublime effect! The middle section, one of the finest examples of working-out extant, is constructed for the most part on an accessory theme. This is the delicious, unforgettable violin melody, to a pizzicato accompaniment, which, transposed from the dominant (the key in which it is first heard) to E-flat major, is now treated as a subject and forms the contrapuntal material. Toward the end this phrase returns in the tonic as a melody with an increase of charm and delight.'

Using no technicalities whatever and with not one quotation, Ulibichev succeeds in giving us a clear idea of the subjects that make up this first movement and of the treatment they undergo. It is an analysis as poetic as it is exact. Moreover, merely in the chapter devoted to the symphonies, many passages of the Russian critic conjure up so vivid an image that it is impressed immediately on the mind, a picture that it is a great pity one cannot reproduce, since it so astonishingly translates and illustrates the musical idea. I cannot resist quoting the following passage dealing with the andante:

'*Andante*, F major, 3/4. Whether a slow movement follows a movement of energetic passion and suffering, or an outburst of jubilation such as the first allegro of this symphony, it always marks that point of repose, of quietude and relaxation, of cessation, which follows great disturbances of the soul. Here the interruption of the ode, the andante, is a picture of calm felicity, of the most profound enchantment. The theme, ravishing in

expression, and as singable as any vocal melody,[45] oc-
cupies less space than Mozart usually accords to the first
subject and its derivatives in the construction of a movement; and this fact attaches importance to the profusion
of accessory ideas, to the number and singular euphony
of the rival motifs. This quantity of beautiful musical
detail, interspersed by long passages in thirty-second
notes and in sextuplets, these phrases multiplied by
themselves in their repetitions and imitations, shed a sort
of twilight over the movement, in which the ear loses
itself with delight, as the eye of a spectator in a thicket
pierced by the rays of the setting sun, illuminating and
inflaming it, peopling it with a thousand fantastic visions. Nevertheless, thick, heavy clouds from time to
time blot out the blue sky; the sharp thorn of grief is felt
in the soul; painful syncopations trouble the harmony;
the minor mode breaks out and dominates the scene, in
a sequence of phrases quivering with fear; but this smoke
without fire, these unsubstantial scarecrows, sport of a
capricious breeze, appear at random and disappear likewise. The sun triumphs over all these feeble portents of
bad weather, his burning disk reappears with the theme,
the heart expands under the rays of an ineffable beati-
tude.'

I cannot think of reproducing here the description of
the finale of the 'Jupiter' given by the author. It must
suffice to mention that for Ulibichev 'the fugue in C is
Mozart's masterpiece in the symphonic genre, and the
highest expression of the genre itself: *der höchste Stand-
punkt*, a German critic has said.' Comparing the C major
Symphony to a musical ode that had achieved the sum-
mits, it is logical, concludes the author, 'that since the

[45] It is the finest example of the *cantabile* in instrumental style.

musical ode could go no farther, Mozart composed no more symphonies.'

With regard to the minuet of this symphony there is an almost universal error in interpretation. As far back as 1843 Ulibichev remarked that 'the composer's lyrical emotion is rekindled to burst out with a furious gaiety in the minuet allegretto, 3/4, which is usually taken allegro.' [46] Some twenty-five years later Richard Wagner said the same thing even more insistently:

'. . . Nevertheless, I believe Haydn's minuets are generally taken too quickly; undoubtedly the minuets of Mozart's symphonies are; this will be felt very distinctly if, for instance, the minuet in Mozart's symphony in G minor, and still more that of his symphony in C major, be played a little slower than at the customary pace. It will be found that the latter minuet which is usually hurried and treated almost as a *Presto*, will now show a quite different character combining grace with impressive strength; in contrast with which, the trio, with its delicately sustained rhythm is reduced, as usually given, to an empty hurry-scurry.' [47]

The insistence with which the composer of *Tristan* discusses the great symphonies of Mozart and the authentic way of interpreting them proves that they alone held in his mind a place worthy of being next to Beethoven's. And that is so true that he notes an analogy between the two themes of the finale of the 'Jupiter' and the opening theme of Beethoven's *Eroica*.' [48] He remarks that these themes scarcely differ from each other, and he presents them in the following order:

[46] Ulibichev, op. cit., Vol. III, p. 263.
[47] Wagner: *The Art of Conducting*, Dannreuther's translation, p. 26.
[48] Ibid.

At the same time he is led to make another comparison, to which I have previously alluded, between the
finale of Mozart's E flat Symphony and that of Beethoven's A major; and for these movements 'wherein
the figuration overwhelms the melody' the opinion of
Wagner is that they 'cannot be taken with too much
decision or swiftness.' [49]

  Can it be said that the foregoing is the last step in what
I have called 'Mozart's symphonic evolution'? At first
sight one would be tempted to believe so. But I shall
have to show that the master pursued his efforts further,
and his conception of orchestral writing during the last
few months of his existence was no longer quite that
which his three great symphonies offer us. The finale of
the 'Jupiter' did perhaps serve as a step toward the instrumental preface to that really extraordinary and, if
one may say so, unclassifiable work, *Die Zauberflöte*.
That Mozart has here written an overture and scenes
that are properly symphonic masterpieces, in the most
modern sense of the word, I need hardly trouble to
prove—if only by the treatment of the woodwind in
particular, and more generally by the way the strings
are united with the wind. But that did not hinder Mozart, hard pressed by circumstances, from writing at
about the same time a symphonic page for the opening

[49] Ibid.

of his drama *La Clemenza di Tito* which still suggests pretty closely the first allegro of the 'Jupiter.' [50] So his great and last symphony remained firmly fixed in his memory despite later changes of style.

It is not possible to pass over in silence a long and heavy task imposed on Mozart by his learned friend Baron van Swieten, which was certainly not without a profound influence on the destiny of his art. Toward the autumn of 1788—one of the most astonishing years for rich productiveness—this wealthy patron took it into his head that, though the oratorios of Handel were things of great beauty, the arias offered a certain monotony to the listener. If these arias were reorchestrated, enhanced by parts for the wind, their musical beauty would be not only more striking but more accessible to the audiences of 1789–90—that is to say, for them more 'modern.' And who better fitted than Mozart to accomplish this task? And pressed by domestic worries and urged on by his natural good nature, Mozart set to work; as early as November 1788 the revision of *Acis and Galatea* was finished. The undertaking occupied nearly two years. In March 1789 it was one of the most famous masterpieces of the older master, *Messiah*, then in July 1790 the *Ode for St. Cecilia's Day* and *Alexander's Feast*.

I shall leave on one side the question of the legitimacy of this revision. It must suffice to say that in 1788–90 no one saw anything incongruous in these retouches, and that van Swieten was guided solely by the desire to revive the whole of Handel's work; as for Mozart, judg-

[50] *La Clemenza di Tito*, commissioned for the coronation of the Emperor Leopold II as King of Bohemia, was produced in Prague on September 6, 1791. (Tr.)

ing by the amount of work accomplished by him, it seems that he quickly acquired a taste for the work, which was after all a more worthy task than was to be reserved for him in the near future. It was in fact during these last years of his life that, deprived of every resource, his court duties compelled him to provide the assembly halls of Vienna with dance tunes; the overburdening task of supplying wind parts to arias from oratorios originally scored for strings only was certainly one quite different for the mind from compiling sets of dances suitable for carnival use in these same years. We have seen Mozart already dipping delightedly into the study of Bach and Handel, at the instigation of van Swieten, at the time of his first Viennese symphony or serenade, in 1782. We see him now for more than two years in direct contact with Handel's work, we might almost say with the composer himself. This is a fact of undeniable importance which we must now take into consideration, since I have said that Mozart's symphonic activity was not cut short even though he wrote no more symphonies.

I do not know that one can easily visualize what the solution of such a problem would be for Mozart, arrived at the climax of his artistic career. It was a question of adorning with all the newly acquired riches the somewhat bare statue of the giant carved in stone about 1740. And in clothing and ornamenting it the same stone had to be used so that no foreign intervention should be apparent. As the major part of Mozart's work rests on the wind instruments, it may perhaps be permissible to suppose that the master's supreme facility and the preference he evinced for these instruments during the last years of his life found in this work a considerable exercise, a food such as perhaps no original creation could have provided. And, moreover, this intercourse with the masters of the past was perhaps already active at the time of the composition of the finale to the 'Jupiter'— without taking into account Mozart's own affinities, which had for a long time been drawing him nearer to the great man, himself no stranger to Italy, in whom the German genius incarnate was not unmixed with a quite different alloy.

The fact is that during the accomplishment of his task as arranger, while he is dispensing the treasures of his contrapuntal science (revivified by contact with Handel); while the woodwind in scintillating variety was re-echoing its brilliance in his ears, and being superposed in vast columns and in complete independence over Handel's string parts; while Mozart was thus trying to enrich the art of the older master with the modern spirit, his own genius was being impregnated, or rather intoxicated, by these ancient sources.

The result, as much in the realm of chamber music as in the orchestral field, was some works wherein counterpoint is woven into the very roots of the work, serving as a canvas for inventions of the richest kind, both extremely bold and solid. Between the truly astounding finale of his last string quartet (June 1790) and the masterly Quintet in D (December of the same year), he passed the whole of the month of July in scoring, "in modern style," Handel's *Alexander's Feast* and the *Ode for St. Cecilia's Day*.

How is it possible not to take account of these facts, and not to see that this work was still echoing in his mind when he wrote the overture and the symphonic ensembles of *Die Zauberflöte*? And when it comes to the final Requiem, this influence becomes visible to the extent of finding a Handelian theme in one of the most famous ensembles of the work! In this is to be seen the fruit of study and contact with one of the greatest and richest masters of all music, a study that served to provide Mozart with one of the last musical satisfactions of his brief existence and to hand down to us the ineffable beauty of the first orchestral page of the Requiem.

We know only too well, alas, what were the mental neglect and material privations of Mozart's last years. His orchestra, between the great symphonies and *Die Zauberflöte*, had to be content to re-echo in the Vienna Redoutensaal, accompanying dances, masked balls, and annual celebrations. There he dedicated to the nobility his series of minuets, and to the more humble classes his German dances and his *Ländler*. One might say that these works, which form real orchestral suites, ending with grand symphonic codas,[51] are almost totally unknown. But, both by the miraculous beauty of their melodies and by the inexhaustible variety and unexpectedness of their 'symphonic' or picturesque strokes of genius,[52] these often represent for us a continuation, quite forgotten, of Mozart's instrumental or orchestral progress. Many a delicious surprise would arise today from a performance of these dances, written for a very

[51] See particularly K.568, 571, 585, 586, 599, 600, 602, 604, 606.

[52] Some recall by their titles political events: war against the Turks, battles; others, fragments of operas then in vogue; others again imitate bizarre instruments, or birds; the trio of one of these is entitled "*Der Kanarienvogel*" ("The Canary"), and would serve as a basis for an admirable symphonic scherzo. Finally, a *Kontretanz* entitled *Les Filles malicieuses* seems to indicate a choreographic program.

large orchestra, with a refinement and a noble, a beautiful poetry, sometimes also with so much simplicity and humor that one might imagine one can already hear the Viennese rhythms of Schubert. In pursuing his humble task, in fulfilling his official mission, Mozart has again, within the limits of a fixed framework, found the means of creating a beauty of an order infinitely superior to what was due in such a case.

There is, too, the fact, rightly noted by Abert,[53] that the juxtaposition of courtly and popular dances in a set of 'carnival redoutes' patronized by the Emperor himself provides almost a replica of the ball scene in *Don Giovanni:* we know with what art and skill the master has contrived to alternate the dances appropriate to every order of society in the salons of the Spanish grandee, and we have the same again here, at a time when the reigning monarch favored the bringing together of the different classes; and if the theater were to present the spectacle of the Viennese dances of 1788 to 1791 we would today, as it were, be attending the festivities contemporaneous with Mozart's last years. And I must repeat that if these dances were set aside or passed over in silence the great picture I have attempted to depict of the various 'curves' of Mozart's symphonic activity would have lacked some of the final colors he planned to give to his great orchestral vision.

But it is abundantly clear that Mozart, now arrived at the last year of his life, has given us the most convincing testimony, the most certain proof of the revolution that has been effected in his thought, in both style and orchestration. In regard to the latter, the overture to *Die*

[53] *W. A. Mozart*, Vol. II, pp. 613 ff.

Zauberflöte in particular [54] offers us the stupendous
example of a work whose form harks back to distant
ages, and whose harmony and scoring suggest an entirely
modern approach; there is no longer the least subordina-
tion of the wind instruments to the strings, but a col-
laboration wherein each fills a most active and appropriate role, a kind of sonorous fullness that Mozart had
not previously achieved, and which opens the most attractive vistas of the future. Furthermore, with the first
orchestral page that serves as a prelude to the Requiem,
the master gives us his last word on his symphonic preoccupations: the return to ancient forms, clothed in
harmonies capable of holding the attention of the most
modern musicians. The unheard-of audacities practiced
in the two Fantasias for a mechanical organ, and the
finale of his last string quartet, with their predilection
for contrapuntal writing, shows us what in general Mozart's latest tendencies were; in terms of the symphony
they are affirmed in the overture to *Die Zauberflöte* and
the first pages of the Requiem; they are of an order so
elevated that they cannot but excite an eternal regret for
the symphony Mozart would surely have written had
God but allowed him a few more months of life.

[54] Concerning Mozart's orchestration at this time see Ulibichev, Vol. III, pp. 414 and 437; Abert, op. cit., Vol. II, pp. 770–5.

CHAPTER FIFTEEN

Josef Haydn and Mozart's Last Symphonies

I WAS BOLD ENOUGH to state at the beginning of the preceding chapter that Mozart's last three symphonic monuments dominated not only his entire work, but all the art of the eighteenth century. When we examine the mass of symphonic output in the classical period, we make a lengthy halt before the most outstanding personality, before him who is generally considered the true and perhaps unique model for Mozart; before Josef Haydn, then arrived at his full maturity. There is no doubt that compared with him a number of his compatriots seem rather small figures; but if, when it came to the question of editing the great edition of his works (still, alas, incomplete), many symphonies that had wrongly figured under his name in the early catalogue had to be eliminated, it seems that a number of his compatriots had written what could actually be mistaken for his own—naturally not the more important or characteristic ones. There were in fact in the Viennese school men whose work was far from negligible, offering interesting specimens of the classical or pre-classical symphony, for the most part from the fecund pen of a Wagenseil: for an example, of symphonies contemporaneous with Mozart's life, those of Johann Vanhall, and of Karl Ditters von Dittersdorf, the inspiration of the former often very curiously romantic, the second most picturesque, furnish interesting pre-Mozartian examples; but it is clear that Haydn's genius, his especially friendly relations with Mozart, and the importance of his own symphonic work, prompt research, which moreover does not seem to have been pushed very far.

If in fact it is asked which exactly are the Haydn symphonies that were expressly used by Mozart as models at the time when he reached the apex of his symphonic art —that is, from 1786 on—it is with some surprise that one establishes the fact that the most famous of the Esterház master's symphonies date from his London visits —that is to say, from a time when Mozart had already departed this life; and naturally the only ones we are specially concerned with here are those written between 1786 and 1788. About a dozen symphonies are extant, of which the first six were destined for some Paris concerts,[1] and the last, known as the 'Oxford,' celebrates Haydn's accession to the doctorate of music in the famous English university in 1788.[2] Among the Parisian symphonies are to be found those named *'L'Ours,' 'La Poule,' 'La Reine de France'* (about 1786), titles which indicate pretty well the need we have always felt for some sort of appellation for pieces of instrumental music.

We might ask whether Mozart knew them, if copies had been able to circulate in Germany before they ap-

[1] The concerts of the Loge Olympique. (Tr.)
[2] The degree of Doctor of Music was conferred on Haydn at Oxford on July 8, 1791. The 'Oxford' Symphony was written for Paris, in 1788. (Tr.)

peared in Paris; it certainly seems that a symphony in E
flat (No.84),[3] from the Paris set, likewise another very
remarkable one in C major (No.90), written about
1787, could not have remained a dead letter for the
great symphonist Mozart had become just at this precise
time; a certain smooth, fluid beauty distinguishes these
symphonies profoundly from those Haydn wrote primarily to amuse the public, and allies them to Mozart in
both the matter of form and the ideas.

But supposing Mozart to have had the chance of reading or hearing one or the other, how can we find, even
in these cases, anything but the framework? Neither
their rapid and charming gaiety, nor the rusticity of
some of the minuets, nor the greater part of their andantes with variations, with the very frequent alternation of major and minor, nor even the piquant animation
of the finales—none of these find enduring echoes in the
four Mozartian monuments built on the same forms and
almost on the same materials. It would be necessary to
probe much further back in Josef Haydn's symphonic
career to meet higher ideals and a greater power of
thought; despite his fifty years, he sailed entirely in the
waters of 'galanterie,' and perhaps the cruel news telling
him of the premature death of his friend, so dear to him,
momentarily gave to his thought something more noble
and elevated.[4]

Again, if Mozart, after 1788, had written only the
Symphony-Serenade of 1782 and the 'Linz' Symphony
(1783), perhaps it would have been possible to speak
with more justification of the determining influence of
Haydn; but the first movement of that symphony-

[3] Numbering according to Breitkopf & Härtel's edition.
[4] See particularly No. 99 (written in 1793).

serenade would certainly have had to be excluded, as it is nothing more than an incisive and audacious *fugato* to which there is nothing equivalent in any Haydn symphony in the period under discussion (1780 to 1790). Haydn's conception, it must be insisted, was at that time far, very far, from Mozart's: and the older master is removed from Mozart, not so much by his orchestral technique, sometimes so elaborate and yet so naturally witty, as by the quality of his ideas and the very depth of his inspiration. Haydn's interior world—since the time of his great 'romantic' crisis noted for the first time by my never to be forgotten master Téodor de Wyzewa,[5] which he had undergone about 1772 or 1773 in the midst of a period of *Sturm und Drang,*—is singularly narrow: we are of course here considering only his symphonic output which, in my opinion, is infinitely surpassed by the last sets of string quartets. In Wyzewa's opinion—since then verified by myself many times— Haydn the symphonist between 1780 and 1790, and again in all his later symphonies written in London in his declining years, with one exception—this Haydn is, first and foremost, an 'entertainer.' A marvelous and inexhaustible entertainer, certainly; a man whose richly flavored and balanced art traces a beautifully poised musical line, linking the soundest learning with the astonishing rusticity of the minuets, revealing itself sometimes in the most unexpected manner in the course of those furious finales that kindle an exultation *sui generis,* to the verge of distraction. A captivating and healthy distraction, with no unwholesome quality about it, which, far from fatiguing, on the contrary freshens and invigorates like open-air exercise. This is the particular

[5] See *Revue des Deux-Mondes,* December 15, 1909.

contribution of Haydn's work contemporaneous with the great symphonies of Mozart. But how can we explain the enormous 'mental' and expressive superiority of the latter?

To us there is no exaggeration in the claim that it is rather the Haydn of the London symphonies (1791–5) who at times recalls Mozart,[6] and the overwhelming influence of Haydn's symphonies on those of Mozart's maturity has perhaps been too readily inferred. If we make a direct comparison of two or three of the 'Parisian' symphonies, written by Haydn in 1786, also two or three others composed in 1787 and 1788, with Mozart's symphonies, what do we find? We see works almost identical in form, but differing profoundly in spirit. None of these Haydn symphonies, however ingenious, witty, or solid they may be, betrays for a single moment any hint of the passion, agitation, or uneasiness by which Mozart's great creative mind reveals itself; we find but rarely that fragrance of warm, youthful tenderness that every work written by Mozart exhales; we can find there none of the signs by which we recognize the gifts of that fertile poetic fancy which yielded Mozart so many unexpected strokes of genius. But we strive in vain to describe two absolutely different inner worlds, which have been wrongly considered as having contributed to the formation of each other. I have not, indeed, attempted a pointless and in fact impossible comparison just in order to lead to the ordinary result of exalting one at the expense of the other; I would even

[6] Particularly that magnificent Symphony in E flat, written between the two London visits (1793), to which I have just alluded, and which is a sort of supreme homage to Mozart's memory.

say that one of the principal features of the real symphonic style—the elaboration of motifs—seems more
richly active in Haydn, and much nearer to Beethoven's
art, than is generally the case with Mozart. But what
slow introduction from Haydn's symphonies could we
honestly compare with the enormous and significant
preludes that open, for instance, Mozart's 'Prague' or E
flat symphonies? What amiable andante of the Esterház
master dare we bring near the romantic visions of the G
minor, of the 'Jupiter'? And what finale of Haydn's can
sustain the splendor of the finales of these two symphonies? As a measure of the unbridgeable gulf between
the art of the two men, contrast Mozart's last symphonic finale with one of the last and most remarkable
of Haydn's, that ending his 'Military' Symphony
(No.100) composed in 1794: although six years later
than the 'Jupiter,' it is quite evident that this finale has
neither the size nor the range of that which concludes
Mozart's greatest symphonic work.

How vain is the attempt to establish kinship when
such a genius inspires such works! Once arrived at its
climax, Mozart's genius, by its very poetic essence and
universality, evades all attempt at *rapprochement*. There
is no common ground between the close of one age and
the beginning of another.

In the symphonic field it would not, however, be
difficult to discover in Mozart certain traces of the influence exerted by Haydn; but it would be necessary to
go back particularly to the period before he came to
settle in Vienna. Moreover, we have already had occasion on a number of preceding pages to note this influence, when we were studying the works written by Mozart during the years 1772–4. There is incontestably a

considerable debt here, contracted by the younger man to the older; but once arrived at full maturity it can be said, in fact, that Mozart draws on himself, and that the treasures of his inner life sufficed him for nourishment. And besides, this treasury of beauty and of poetry is so rich and deep that it seems there was no one among his contemporaries at that time with the power to offer him anything of equal value. Most of these spoke the same language, but without his genius. Even when we examine the symphonies written by Haydn between 1784 and 1788, for example, we certainly cannot see in them the inspiring model of Mozart's great symphonies. The latter, considered solely from the harmonic viewpoint, are portals opening on the future: the imposing opening of the E flat Symphony, with its harsh and bold modulations, the mysterious andante of the G minor Symphony, the minor passages in the andante cantabile of the 'Jupiter,' belong already to the following age, and even presage Wagner; while in comparison the symphonic work of old Haydn, with very rare exceptions, serves as a conclusion to the instrumental art of the eighteenth century. This 'modernism' of Mozart has been appreciated only quite recently; there is decidedly an evolution in the mode of appraising and performing the work of great men: the harmonic boldnesses, so easy to establish, so frequent in the composer of *Die Zauberflöte*, had been observed only rarely before the time of Fétis, who proposed to correct the introduction of the last of the 'Haydn' Quartets. And the same observation might be made with regard to the poetic essence, the universality of human feeling, always stamped with the same formal beauty, which we are beginning to discover in Mozart. It is not so long since critics took it into their heads to compare Mozart to Shakespeare, and that marks a date; perhaps even the special enthusiasm that Mozart prompts in some writers of the younger generation of today proceeds a little from this universal character of his genius—a genius that has no fear of the ridiculous even when it borders on the sublime. No position is more false than that which admits only a certain order of invariable beauty in Mozart's work; one is astonished to see today all the feelings of the human soul in contact with life reflected therein with, in addition, the feeling surpassing all others, that of the mystery of the beyond.

Mozart's last symphonies, then, form a whole that in my opinion dominates all the production of the classical period, including the remarkable work—often unique in its own genre—of Josef Haydn. I have no doubt whatever that Mozart's last symphonies aim at a higher mark than any others that were written in the period of his maturity; not by any means that they speak a different language, or that they were conceived in a revolutionary spirit, tending to repudiate the past and erect something in its place. They spring solely from a brilliant mind, from a man whose inner world surpassed all in richness, in expression, and in beauty; Mozart's power of clothing all things from the greatest to the smallest in this beauty remained essentially the privilege of the poet he always was. And he had no need to turn things topsy-turvy, putting the end before the beginning, in order to create novelty; it was only necessary for him to fill the framework with his own thought for everything to be rejuvenated. In the same way the richness and variety of the contrasts with which his work is filled come out more and more clearly today, completely reversing the usual judgments relative to his art conceded

by the romantic age: [7] they proceed from his very special aptitude for observing mankind in all the varied
manifestations of life, for grasping a foreign tongue,
down to the least inflection, with an alertness and delicacy rare among his compatriots. This is not the least of
our surprises in the presence of Mozart; it is evident that
throughout almost the whole of his life he had the clearest appreciation of Italian *buffa* art, whose technique
was appropriated by him to a degree unexampled and
unforeseeable; it was not only the formal beauty of the
Italian musical phrase as adopted sentimentally by a
Christian Bach, but a leaning toward the most biting and
delicate satire, which, indeed, was quite in keeping with
his own character. On reflection one realizes that he
even surpasses his model by the full extent of his own
genius, and, as Abert has so justly remarked, Mozart
seems to smile on the personages he creates, but who,
one feels, are so very different from him.

Commentators have been specially led to analyze
these marvelous gifts in the stage works. I have wished
to be sufficiently discerning to attempt to illustrate them
from his instrumental works, and particularly here in his
great symphonies. The latter seem to me the most absolute witness, the most intimate revelations of his 'ego';
and I feel that a long companionship with such masterpieces has not sufficed to reveal all the treasures of their
profound and moving beauty. As with all great creators,
the secret of this beauty is not fully revealed at first
sight; however, we cannot help being astonished that it
has needed nearly a century and a half for people to
discover in Mozart anything other than grace and

[7] See the psychological analysis of Mozart's personality already
noted above: Abert, op. cit., Vol. II, pp. 1–36.

charming elegance. This miraculous artist, as Téodor de Wyzewa used to style him, in his last symphonies does in fact reveal to us the true world inhabited by his soul at the moment when it is turning toward other regions. The fact is that from 1789 or 1790 the very source of Mozart's inspiration changes; a sort of purification, accompanied often by a feeling of resigned lassitude, gives to his work a beauty removed from all passion, purged of all anxiety, testifying to an almost celestial calm. His last three symphonies seem definitely to set the seal on the most 'romantic' period of all his career, in which the ardent tumult of life is quelled only to allow him time to ascend to even higher regions.

Appendix

Bibliography

Index

APPENDIX

A List of the Symphonic Works of Mozart

(The dates given in this list, which differ in some respects from those in
the body of the work, are taken from Einstein's revision of Köchel's

KÖCHEL NUMBER	SYMPHONY	SCORING	DATE AND PLACE OF COMPOSITION
16	No. 1	in E flat, 2 vlns, vla, bass, 2 oboes, 2 horns	London, 1764 or early 1765
17 (Anh. 223a)	No. 2	in B flat, 2 vlns, vla, bass, 2 oboes, 2 horns	London, 1764 or early 1765
18 (Anh. 109i)	No. 3	in E flat, 2 vlns, vla, bass, 2 clts, 2 horns, bassoon	London (copied), 1764
19	No. 4	in D, 2 vlns, vla, bass, 2 oboes, 2 horns	London, 1765
22	No. 5	in B flat, 2 vlns, vla, bass, 2 oboes, 2 horns	The Hague, Dec. 1765
43	No. 6	in F, 2 vlns, vla, bass, 2 oboes, 2 horns (oboes replaced by flutes in the Andante)	Vienna-Olmütz, Dec. 1767
45	No. 7	in D, 2 vlns, vla, bass, 2 oboes, 2 horns, tpts, kettledrums	Vienna, Jan. 16, 1768
48	No. 8	in D, 2 vlns, vla, bass, 2 oboes, 2 horns, tpts, kettledrums	Vienna, Dec. 13, 1768
73 (75a)	No. 9	in C, 2 vlns, vla, bass, 2 oboes, 2 horns, tpts, kettledrums	Salzburg, summer 1771
74	No. 10	in G, 2 vlns, vla, bass, 2 oboes, 2 horns	Milan, Dec. 1770
75	No. 42	in F, 2 vlns, vla, bass, 2 oboes, 2 horns	Salzburg, 1771
76 (42a)	No. 43	in F, 2 vlns, vla, bass, 2 oboes, 2 horns, 2 bassoons	Vienna, autumn 1767
81 (73l)	No. 44	in D, 2 vlns, vla, bass, 2 oboes, 2 horns	Rome, April 25, 1770

catalogue [1937]. Where his revised numbers differ from those of Köchel's original classification, these are given in brackets alongside the original.)

[1] Those symphonies where no date is given were first published in Breitkopf & Härtel's complete edition of Mozart's works.

KÖCHEL NUMBER	SYM- PHONY	SCORING	DATE AND PLACE OF COMPOSITION
84 (73q)	No. 11	in D, 2 vlns, vla, bass, 2 oboes, 2 horns	Milan and Bologna, 1770
95 (73n)	No. 45	in D, 2 vlns, vla, bass, 2 oboes, 2 horns, 2 tpts	Rome, April 25, 1770
96 (111b)	No. 46	in C, 2 vlns, vla, bass, 2 oboes, 2 horns, 2 tpts, kettledrums	Milan, Oct.- Nov. 1771
97 (73m)	No. 47	in D, 2 vlns, vla, bass, 2 oboes, 2 horns, 2 tpts, kettledrums	Rome, April 1770
98 (Anh. 223b)	No. 48	in F, 2 vlns, vla, bass, 2 oboes, 2 horns	Milan?, 1771
99 (63a)		Cassation in B flat, 2 vlns, vla, bass, 2 oboes, 2 horns	Salzburg, summer 1769
100 (62a)		Serenade in D, 2 vlns, vla, bass, 2 horns, 1 tpt, 2 oboes	Salzburg, summer 1769
110 (75b)	No. 12	in G, 2 vlns, vla, bass, 2 oboes, 2 horns (2 flutes and 2 bassoons in the Andante)	Salzburg, July 1771
112	No. 14	in F, 2 vlns, vla, bass, 2 oboes, 2 horns	Milan, Nov. 2, 1771
114	No. 14	in A, 2 vlns, vla, bass, 2 flutes, 2 horns	Salzburg, Dec. 30, 1771
124	No. 15	in G, 2 vlns, vla, bass, 2 oboes, 2 horns	Salzburg, Feb. 2, 1772
128	No. 16	in C, 2 vlns, vla, bass, 2 oboes, 2 horns	Salzburg, May 1772
129	No. 17	In G, 2 vlns, vla, bass, 2 oboes, 2 horns	Salzburg, May 1772
130	No. 18	in F, 2 vlns, vla, bass, 2 flutes, 2 horns (in F), 2 horns (in C)	Salzburg, May 1772

APPENDIX

SYM-PHONY	FIRST EDITION	NUMBER OF MOVEMENTS	REFERENCE PAGE
No. 11		3. Allegro—Andante—Allegro	25
No. 45		4. Allegro—Andante—Menuetto—Allegro	24
No. 46		4. Allegro—Andante—Menuetto—Allegro molto	37–9
No. 47		4. Allegro—Andante—Menuetto—Presto	24
No. 48		4. Allegro—Andante—Menuetto—Presto	27–8
		7. Marcia—Allegro molto—Andante—Menuetto—Andante—Menuetto—Allegro	13–14
		8. Allegro—Andante—Menuetto—Allegro—Menuetto—Andante—Menuetto—Allegro	13–14
No. 12		4. Allegro—Andante—Menuetto—Allegro	27–8
No. 14		4. Allegro—Andante—Menuetto—Molto Allegro (Rondeau)	27–9
No. 14		4. Allegro moderato—Andante—Menuetto—Molto Allegro	31–2
No. 15		4. Allegro—Andante—Menuetto—Presto (Rondeau)	31–2
No. 16		3. Allegro maestoso—Andantino grazioso—Allegro (Rondeau)	33
No. 17		3. Allegro—Andante—Allegro	33
No. 18		4. Allegro—Andantino grazioso—Menuetto—Molto Allegro	34

KÖCHEL NUMBER	SYM- PHONY	SCORING	DATE AND PLACE OF COMPOSITION
132	No. 19	in E flat, 2 vlns, vla, bass, 2 oboes, 4 horns (E flat)	Salzburg, July 1772
133	No. 20	in D, 2 vlns, vla, bass, 2 oboes, 2 horns, tpts (flute obbligato in the Andante)	Salzburg, July 1772
134	No. 21	in A, 2 vlns, vla, bass, 2 flutes, 2 horns	Salzburg, Aug. 1772
162	No. 22	in C, 2 vlns, vla, bass, 2 oboes, 2 horns, 2 tpts	Salzburg, autumn 1773
181 (162b)	No. 23	in D, 2 vlns, vla, bass, 2 oboes, 2 horns, 2 tpts	Salzburg, May 1773
182 (166c)	No. 24	in B flat, 2 vlns, vla, bass, 2 oboes, 2 horns	Salzburg, May or June 1773
183	No. 25	in G minor, 2 vlns, vla, bass, 2 horns (in G), 2 horns (in B flat), 2 bassoons	Salzburg, end of 1773
184 (166a)	No. 26	in E flat, 2 vlns, vla, bass, 2 oboes, 2 bassoons, 2 horns, 2 tpts	Salzburg, autumn 1773
199 (162a)	No. 27	in G, 2 vlns, vla, bass, 2 flutes, 2 horns	Salzburg, April 1773
200 (173e)	No. 28	in C, 2 vlns, vla, bass, 2 oboes, 2 horns, 1 bassoon, 2 tpts	Salzburg, Nov. 1773
201 (186a)	No. 29	in A, 2 vlns, vla, bass, 2 oboes, 2 horns	Salzburg, early 1774
202 (186b)	No. 30	in D, 2 vlns, vla, bass, 2 oboes, 2 horns, 2 tpts	Salzburg, May 5, 1774
239		*Serenata notturna* in D, string quartet and string orchestra, kettledrums	Salzburg, Jan. 1776

SYM-PHONY	FIRST EDITION	NUMBER OF MOVEMENTS	REFER-ENCE PAGE
No. 19		5. Allegro—Andante—Menuetto—Allegro (Rondeau)—Andantino grazioso	31, 34–5
No. 20		4. Allegro—Andante—Menuetto—Allegro	32–3, 36
No. 21		4. Allegro—Andante—Menuetto—Allegro	35
No. 22	Günther & Böhme (Hamburg), *Quatre Symphonies.* Op. 64. no. 1. 1798	3. Allegro assai—Andantino grazioso—Presto assai	42–3
No. 23		3. Allegro spiritoso—Andantino grazioso—Presto assai	42–3
No. 24		3. Allegro spiritoso—Andantino grazioso—Allegro (Rondo)	42–3
No. 25	Günther & Böhme (Hamburg). Op. 64. no. II. 1798	4. Allegro con brio—Andante—Menuetto—Allegro	48–51
No. 26		3. Molto Presto—Andante—Allegro (Rondo)	40–2
No. 27	Günther & Böhme (Hamburg). Op. 64. no. III. 1799	3. Allegro—Andantino grazioso—Presto	47
No. 28		4. Allegro spiritoso—Andante—Menuetto—Presto	48–51
No. 29		4. Allegro moderato—Andante—Menuetto—Allegro con spirito	48–51
No. 30	Günther & Böhme (Hamburg). Op. 64. no. IV. 1799	4. Molto Allegro—Andantino con moto—Menuetto—Presto	48–51
		3. Marcia. Maestoso—Menuetto—Rondeau. Allegretto	59–60

KÖCHEL NUMBER	SYM-PHONY	SCORING	DATE AND PLACE OF COMPOSITION
250 (248b)		Serenade in D, 2 vlns, vla, bass, 2 oboes, 2 bassoons, 2 horns, 2 tpts	Salzburg, July 1776
286 (269a)		*Notturno*, in D, for 4 orchestras, each of 2 vlns, vla, bass, 2 horns	Salzburg, Dec. 1776 to Jan. 1777
297 (300a)	No. 31	in D, 2 vlns, vla, bass, 2 flutes, 2 oboes, 2 clts, 2 bassoons, 2 horns, 2 tpts, kettledrums	Paris, June 12, 1778
318	No. 32	in G, 2 vlns, vla, bass, 2 flutes, 2 oboes, 2 bassoons, 4 horns, 2 tpts	Salzburg, April 26, 1779
319	No. 33	in B flat, 2 vlns, vla, bass, 2 oboes, 2 bassoons, 2 horns	Salzburg, July 9, 1779
320		Serenade in D, 2 vlns, vla, bass, 2 flutes, 2 oboes, 2 bassoons, 2 horns, 2 tpts, kettledrums (posthorn in 2nd Menuetto)	Salzburg, Aug. 3, 1779
338	No. 34	in C, 2 vlns, vla, bass, 2 oboes, 2 bassoons, 2 horns, tpts, kettledrums	Salzburg, Aug. 29, 1780
364 (320d)		Concertante for violin and viola, in E flat, 2 vlns, vla, bass, 2 oboes, 2 horns	Salzburg, summer 1779
385	No. 35	in D, 2 vlns, vla, bass, 2 oboes, 2 horns, 2 bassoons, tpts, kettledrums	Vienna, July-Aug. 1782
425	No. 36	in C, 2 vlns, vla, bass, 2 oboes, 2 horns, 2 bassoons, tpts, kettledrums	Linz, Nov. 3, 1783
444 (425a)	No. 37	in G, 2 vlns, vla, bass, 2 oboes, 2 horns (flute extra in Andante)	Adagio added, Linz, Nov. 1783

SYM-PHONY	FIRST EDITION	NUMBER OF MOVEMENTS	REFER-ENCE PAGE
		10. Allegro maestoso—Allegro molto—Andante—Menuetto —Rondo—Menuetto galante —Andante—Menuetto— Adagio—Allegro assai	57-8
		3. Andante—Allegretto grazioso—Menuetto	60
No. 31	Sieber (Paris) 1789	3. Allegro assai—Andantino— Allegro	67-9, 73
No. 32	Imbault (Paris) before 1792	2. Allegro spiritoso—Andante	77-8, 81, 83
No. 33	Artaria (Vienna) 1785	4. Allegro assai—Andante moderato—Menuetto— Finale. Allegro assai	79-80
	André (Offenbach). Op. 22. 1792	7. Adagio. Maestoso—Allegro con spirito—Menuetto— Concertante. Andante grazioso—Andantino—Menuetto —Finale	80-1
No. 34	André (Offenbach). Op. 57. 1797	3. Allegro vivace—Andante di molto—Finale. Allegro vivace	83-5
	André (Offenbach). Op. 104. 1801	3. Allegro maestoso—Andante —Presto	81-3
No. 35	Artaria (Vienna) 1785	4. Allegro con spirito—Andante—Menuetto—Finale —Presto	88-90, 192-3
No. 36	André (Offenbach). Op. 34. 1793	4. Adagio. Allegro spiritoso— Poco Adagio—Menuetto— Presto	91-4, 192
No. 37		3. Adagio. [Allegro con spirito —Andante sostenuto— Allegro molto]	94-5

KÖCHEL NUMBER	SYM- PHONY	SCORING	DATE AND PLACE OF COMPOSITION
477 (479a)		C minor, *Maurerische Trauermusik*, 2 vlns, vla, bass, 2 oboes, 1 clt, 2 horns, 3 basset horns, 1 double bassoon	Vienna, Nov. 10, 1785
504	No. 38	in D, 2 vlns, vla, bass, 2 flutes, 2 oboes, 2 bassoons, 2 horns, tpts, kettledrums	Vienna, Dec. 6, 1786
522		in F, 2 vlns, vla, bass, 2 horns	Vienna, June 14, 1787
543	No. 39	in E flat, 2 vlns, vla, bass, 1 flute, 2 clts, 2 bassoons, 2 horns, 2 tpts, kettledrums	Vienna, June 26, 1788
550	No. 40	in G minor, 2 vlns, vla, bass, 1 flute, 2 bassoons, 2 horns	Vienna, July 25, 1788
551	No. 41	in C, 2 vlns, vla, bass, 1 flute, 2 oboes, 2 bassoons, 2 horns, 2 tpts, kettledrums	Vienna, Aug. 10, 1788

✿   ✿   ✿   ✿

APPENDIX

SYM-PHONY	FIRST EDITION	NUMBER OF MOVEMENTS	REFER-ENCE PAGE
	André (Offenbach). Op. 114. About 1805	1. Adagio	95–6
No. 38	André (Offenbach). Op. 84. 1800	3. Adagio. Allegro—Andante —Finale. Presto	97–101, 195
No. 39	André (Offenbach). Op. 93. About 1801	4. Allegro—Menuetto. Maestoso—Adagio cantabile—Presto	102–4
	André (Offenbach). Op. 58. 1797	4. Adagio. Allegro—Andante con moto—Menuetto. Allegretto—Finale. Allegro	84, 105–6, 111–29, 141, 153–4, 176, 183, 195–6, 199
No. 40	André (Offenbach). Op. 45. 1794	4. Molto Allegro—Andante—Menuetto. Allegretto—Allegro assai	106–11, 124–5, 129–55, 165–6, 176, 195–6, 199
No. 41	André (Offenbach). Op. 38. 1793	4. Allegro vivace—Andante cantabile—Menuetto. Allegretto—Molto Allegro	90, 106, 108–9, 111, 125, 154, 155–86, 195–6, 199

✿   ✿   ✿   ✿

KÖCHEL NUMBER	SCORING	DATE AND PLACE OF COMPOSITION
Anh. 8 (311a)	Overture in B flat, 2 vlns, vla, bass, 2 flutes, 2 oboes, 2 clts, 2 bassoons, 2 horns, 2 tpts, kettle-drums	Paris, Aug.–Sept. 1778
Anh. 9 (297b)	in E flat, 2 vlns, vla, bass, 2 oboes, 2 horns	Paris, April 5–20, 1778
Anh. 100 (383g)	in E flat, 2 vlns, vla, bass, flute, 2 oboes, 2 horns, bassoon	Vienna, spring 1787
Anh. 214 (45b)	in B flat, 2 vlns, vla, bass, 2 oboes, 2 horns	Vienna, early 1768
Anh. 215 (66c)	lost	Salzburg, end of 1769
Anh. 216 (74g)	in B flat, 2 vlns, vla, bass, 2 oboes, 2 horns	Salzburg, 1771
Anh. 217 (66d)	lost	Salzburg, end of 1769
Anh. 218 (66e)	lost	Salzburg, end of 1769
Anh. 221 (45a)	in G, 2 vlns, vla, bass, 2 oboes, 2 horns	Vienna, early 1768

FIRST EDITION	NUMBER OF MOVEMENTS	REFER- ENCE PAGE
L'Imprimerie du Conservatoire (Paris), about 1805	1. Andante & Allegro conspirito spirituoso	70–5
Unpublished	3. Allegro—Adagio—Andantino con variazione	64–5
Unpublished	2. Andante—Allegro	124
Unpublished	4. Allegro—Andante—Menuetto—Allegro	27
Unpublished	—	27
Breitkopf & Härtel (Leipzig). Apr. 1910	4. Allegro—Andante—Menuetto—Allegro molto	27–8
Unpublished	—	27
Unpublished	—	27
Unpublished	3. Allegro maestoso—Andante—Presto	16–18

Bibliography

ABERT, HERMANN: *W. A. Mozart* (5th edition of Otto Jahn's *Mozart*). Leipzig: Breitkopf & Härtel; 1921. 2 vols. See, on the symphonies, Vol. II, pp. 398–401, 567–603.

AMBROS, A. W.: *Grenzen der Poesie und der Musik.* 1856. On the Symphony in E flat, p. 123.

APEL, A.: 'Poem on the E flat Symphony (called Swan Song).' *Allgemeine Musikalische-Zeitung,* Vol. VIII, pp. 453–7, 465–70.

BACHER, OTTO: '*Ein Mozartfund.*' *Zeitschrift für Musikwissenschaft,* January 1926, pp. 226 ff.

BRENET, MICHEL (Marie Bobillier): *Histoire de la symphonie à orchestre jusqu'à Beethoven.* 1882.

BOTSTIBER, H.: *Geschichte der Ouvertüre.* Leipzig, 1913.

CACATRIX: *Correspondance des amateurs musiciens.* 1802–5.

CURZON, H. DE: *Lettres de Mozart* (translated into French). 1888 and 1898. 2 vols.

DELDEVEZ, M. E.: *Curiosités musicales.* 1873.

ELWART, A. A. E.: *Histoire de la Société des Concerts du Conservatoire.* 1860.

FÉTIS, F. J.: *Biographie universelle des musiciens.* 1837–44.

FRAMERY, N. É., and GINGUENÉ, P. L.: *Encyclopédie méthodique,* see Momigny.

GAIL, J.: *Réflexions sur le goût musical en France.*

HOFFMANN, E. T. A.: *Fantasiestücke* (1814), Vol. I, p. 4.

JAHN, OTTO: *W. A. Mozart.* 4 editions: 1856–9, 1867, 1889–91, 1905–7. Leipzig: Breitkopf & Härtel.

KRETZSCHMAR, A. F. H.: *Führer durch den Konzertsaal.* 2

vols. Leipzig, 1913. See, on the Mozart symphonies, Vol. II, pp. 168–89.

KÖCHEL, LUDWIG, RITTER VON: *Chronologisch-thematisches Verzeichnis*. 1st edition, 1862; 2nd edition (revised by Paul, Graf von Waldersee), 1905.

LAURENCIE, LIONEL DE LA: *Le Goût musical en France*, see p. 235.

MENDELSSOHN, FELIX: *Letters, 1833–47.*

MOMIGNY, JEROME JOSEPH DE: *Encyclopédie méthodique*, Vol. II (1818), p. 412 (analysis of the G minor Symphony).

NAEGELI, H. G.: *Vorlesungen über Musik*. 1826.

NEF, KARL: *Geschichte der Sinfonie und Suite*. 1921. See pp. 163–7.

NISSEN, G. N. VON: *Biographie W. A. Mozarts*. 1828.

SCHULTZ, DETLEF: *Mozarts Jugend-Sinfonien*. Leipzig, 1900.

SCHUMANN, ROBERT: *Gesammelte Schriften*, Vol. IV, p. 62 (on a passage in the G minor Symphony).

ULIBICHEV, ALEXANDRE: *Nouvelle Biographie de Mozart*. Moscow, 1843. Vol. III, pp. 233–71.

WAGNER, RICHARD: *The Art-Work of the Future.—On a German School of Music.—The Art of Conducting.— A Happy Evening.—Autobiographical Sketch*. In *Richard Wagner's Prose Works* (8 vols.), English translation (1892–9) by W. Ashton Ellis of the *Gesammelte Schriften*.

WILDER, VICTOR: *Mozart, l'homme et l'artiste*. 1881.

WYZEWA, TÉODOR DE, and SAINT-FOIX, GEORGES DE: *W. A. Mozart, sa vie et son œuvre, de l'enfance à la pleine maturité*. 2 vols. Paris: Perrin; 1912. Completed by Saint-Foix alone (Vols. III–V, 1936–45).

PERIODICALS

Mozart-Jahrbuch. 1st year, 1923. Article by Wilhelm Fischer, pp. 35–69.

Allgemeine Musikalische-Zeitung. 1798 et seq.

Journal de Paris. 1777–9.

Mercure de France. 1777–9.

La Décade philosophique. September 1807.

Tablettes de Polymnie. 1810–11.

Revue musicale. 1828.

La Gazette musicale. 1836–44.

Musikführer:

   No. 8. August Gluck: *W. A. Mozarts G moll Symphonie.* (1788).

   No. 54. A. Pochammer: *W. A. Mozarts Symphonie in C dur.*

   No. 69. C. Witting: *W. A. Mozarts Symphonie in Es dur.*

Index

A CATALOGUE OF SELECTED DOVER BOOKS
IN ALL FIELDS OF INTEREST

A CATALOGUE OF SELECTED DOVER BOOKS
IN ALL FIELDS OF INTEREST

WHAT IS SCIENCE?, *N. Campbell*
The role of experiment and measurement, the function of mathematics, the nature of scientific laws, the difference between laws and theories, the limitations of science, and many similarly provocative topics are treated clearly and without technicalities by an eminent scientist. "Still an excellent introduction to scientific philosophy," H. Margenau in *Physics Today*. "A first-rate primer . . . deserves a wide audience," *Scientific American*. 192pp. 5⅜ x 8.
Paperbound $1.25

THE NATURE OF LIGHT AND COLOUR IN THE OPEN AIR, *M. Minnaert*
Why are shadows sometimes blue, sometimes green, or other colors depending on the light and surroundings? What causes mirages? Why do multiple suns and moons appear in the sky? Professor Minnaert explains these unusual phenomena and hundreds of others in simple, easy-to-understand terms based on optical laws and the properties of light and color. No mathematics is required but artists, scientists, students, and everyone fascinated by these "tricks" of nature will find thousands of useful and amazing pieces of information. Hundreds of observational experiments are suggested which require no special equipment. 200 illustrations; 42 photos. xvi + 362pp. 5⅜ x 8.
Paperbound $2.00

THE STRANGE STORY OF THE QUANTUM, AN ACCOUNT FOR THE GENERAL READER OF THE GROWTH OF IDEAS UNDERLYING OUR PRESENT ATOMIC KNOWLEDGE, *B. Hoffmann*
Presents lucidly and expertly, with barest amount of mathematics, the problems and theories which led to modern quantum physics. Dr. Hoffmann begins with the closing years of the 19th century, when certain trifling discrepancies were noticed, and with illuminating analogies and examples takes you through the brilliant concepts of Planck, Einstein, Pauli, Broglie, Bohr, Schroedinger, Heisenberg, Dirac, Sommerfeld, Feynman, etc. This edition includes a new, long postscript carrying the story through 1958. "Of the books attempting an account of the history and contents of our modern atomic physics which have come to my attention, this is the best," H. Margenau, Yale University, in *American Journal of Physics*. 32 tables and line illustrations. Index. 275pp. 5⅜ x 8.
Paperbound $1.75

GREAT IDEAS OF MODERN MATHEMATICS: THEIR NATURE AND USE, *Jagjit Singh*
Reader with only high school math will understand main mathematical ideas of modern physics, astronomy, genetics, psychology, evolution, etc. better than many who use them as tools, but comprehend little of their basic structure. Author uses his wide knowledge of non-mathematical fields in brilliant exposition of differential equations, matrices, group theory, logic, statistics, problems of mathematical foundations, imaginary numbers, vectors, etc. Original publication. 2 appendixes. 2 indexes. 65 ills. 322pp. 5⅜ x 8.
Paperbound $2.00

THE PRINCIPLES OF PSYCHOLOGY,
William James
The full long-course, unabridged, of one of the great classics of Western literature and science. Wonderfully lucid descriptions of human mental activity, the stream of thought, consciousness, time perception, memory, imagination, emotions, reason, abnormal phenomena, and similar topics. Original contributions are integrated with the work of such men as Berkeley, Binet, Mills, Darwin, Hume, Kant, Royce, Schopenhauer, Spinoza, Locke, Descartes, Galton, Wundt, Lotze, Herbart, Fechner, and scores of others. All contrasting interpretations of mental phenomena are examined in detail—introspective analysis, philosophical interpretation, and experimental research. "A classic," *Journal of Consulting Psychology.* "The main lines are as valid as ever," *Psychoanalytical Quarterly.* "Standard reading . . . a classic of interpretation," *Psychiatric Quarterly.* 94 illustrations. 1408pp. 5⅜ x 8.
Vol. 1 Paperbound $2.50, Vol. 2 Paperbound $2.50,
The set $5.00

VISUAL ILLUSIONS: THEIR CAUSES, CHARACTERISTICS AND APPLICATIONS,
M. Luckiesh
"Seeing is deceiving," asserts the author of this introduction to virtually every type of optical illusion known. The text both describes and explains the principles involved in color illusions, figure-ground, distance illusions, etc. 100 photographs, drawings and diagrams prove how easy it is to fool the sense: circles that aren't round, parallel lines that seem to bend, stationary figures that seem to move as you stare at them — illustration after illustration strains our credulity at what we see. Fascinating book from many points of view, from applications for artists, in camouflage, etc. to the psychology of vision. New introduction by William Ittleson, Dept. of Psychology, Queens College. Index. Bibliography. xxi + 252pp. 5⅜ x 8½.   Paperbound $1.50

FADS AND FALLACIES IN THE NAME OF SCIENCE,
Martin Gardner
This is the standard account of various cults, quack systems, and delusions which have masqueraded as science: hollow earth fanatics, Reich and orgone sex energy, dianetics, Atlantis, multiple moons, Forteanism, flying saucers, medical fallacies like iridiagnosis, zone therapy, etc. A new chapter has been added on Bridey Murphy, psionics, and other recent manifestations in this field. This is a fair, reasoned appraisal of eccentric theory which provides excellent inoculation against cleverly masked nonsense. "Should be read by everyone, scientist and non-scientist alike," R. T. Birge, Prof. Emeritus of Physics, Univ. of California; Former President, American Physical Society. Index. x + 365pp. 5⅜ x 8.   Paperbound $1.85

ILLUSIONS AND DELUSIONS OF THE SUPERNATURAL AND THE OCCULT,
D. H. Rawcliffe
Holds up to rational examination hundreds of persistent delusions including crystal gazing, automatic writing, table turning, mediumistic trances, mental healing, stigmata, lycanthropy, live burial, the Indian Rope Trick, spiritualism, dowsing, telepathy, clairvoyance, ghosts, ESP, etc. The author explains and exposes the mental and physical deceptions involved, making this not only an exposé of supernatural phenomena, but a valuable exposition of characteristic types of abnormal psychology. Originally titled "The Psychology of the Occult." 14 illustrations. Index. 551pp. 5⅜ x 8.   Paperbound $2.25

FAIRY TALE COLLECTIONS, *edited by Andrew Lang*
Andrew Lang's fairy tale collections make up the richest shelf-full of traditional children's stories anywhere available. Lang supervised the translation of stories from all over the world—familiar European tales collected by Grimm, animal stories from Negro Africa, myths of primitive Australia, stories from Russia, Hungary, Iceland, Japan, and many other countries. Lang's selection of translations are unusually high; many authorities consider that the most familiar tales find their best versions in these volumes. All collections are richly decorated and illustrated by H. J. Ford and other artists.

THE BLUE FAIRY BOOK. 37 stories. 138 illustrations. ix + 390pp. 5⅜ x 8½.
Paperbound $1.50

THE GREEN FAIRY BOOK. 42 stories. 100 illustrations. xiii + 366pp. 5⅜ x 8½.
Paperbound $1.50

THE BROWN FAIRY BOOK. 32 stories. 50 illustrations, 8 in color. xii + 350pp. 5⅜ x 8½.
Paperbound $1.50

THE BEST TALES OF HOFFMANN, *edited by E. F. Bleiler*
10 stories by E. T. A. Hoffmann, one of the greatest of all writers of fantasy. The tales include "The Golden Flower Pot," "Automata," "A New Year's Eve Adventure," "Nutcracker and the King of Mice," "Sand-Man," and others. Vigorous characterizations of highly eccentric personalities, remarkably imaginative situations, and intensely fast pacing has made these tales popular all over the world for 150 years. Editor's introduction. 7 drawings by Hoffmann. xxxiii + 419pp. 5⅜ x 8½.
Paperbound $2.00

GHOST AND HORROR STORIES OF AMBROSE BIERCE,
edited by E. F. Bleiler
Morbid, eerie, horrifying tales of possessed poets, shabby aristocrats, revived corpses, and haunted malefactors. Widely acknowledged as the best of their kind between Poe and the moderns, reflecting their author's inner torment and bitter view of life. Includes "Damned Thing," "The Middle Toe of the Right Foot," "The Eyes of the Panther," "Visions of the Night," "Moxon's Master," and over a dozen others. Editor's introduction. xxii + 199pp. 5⅜ x 8½.
Paperbound $1.25

THREE GOTHIC NOVELS, *edited by E. F. Bleiler*
Originators of the still popular Gothic novel form, influential in ushering in early 19th-century Romanticism. Horace Walpole's *Castle of Otranto*, William Beckford's *Vathek*, John Polidori's *The Vampyre*, and a *Fragment* by Lord Byron are enjoyable as exciting reading or as documents in the history of English literature. Editor's introduction. xi + 291pp. 5⅜ x 8½.
Paperbound $2.00

BEST GHOST STORIES OF LEFANU, *edited by E. F. Bleiler*
Though admired by such critics as V. S. Pritchett, Charles Dickens and Henry James, ghost stories by the Irish novelist Joseph Sheridan LeFanu have never become as widely known as his detective fiction. About half of the 16 stories in this collection have never before been available in America. Collection includes "Carmilla" (perhaps the best vampire story ever written), "The Haunted Baronet," "The Fortunes of Sir Robert Ardagh," and the classic "Green Tea." Editor's introduction. 7 contemporary illustrations. Portrait of LeFanu. xii + 467pp. 5⅜ x 8.
Paperbound $2.00

A SHORT ACCOUNT OF THE HISTORY OF MATHEMATICS,
W. W. Rouse Ball
Last previous edition (1908) hailed by mathematicians and laymen for lucid
overview of math as living science, for understandable presentation of individual contributions of great mathematicians. Treats lives, discoveries of every
important school and figure from Egypt, Phoenicia to late nineteenth century.
Greek schools of Ionia, Cyzicus, Alexandria, Byzantium, Pythagoras; primitive
arithmetic; Middle Ages and Renaissance, including European and Asiatic contributions; modern math of Descartes, Pascal, Wallis, Huygens, Newton, Euler,
Lambert, Laplace, scores more. More emphasis on historical development,
exposition of ideas than other books on subject. Non-technical, readable text
can be followed with no more preparation than high-school algebra. Index.
544pp. 5⅜ x 8. Paperbound $2.25

GREAT IDEAS AND THEORIES OF MODERN COSMOLOGY, Jagjit Singh
Companion volume to author's popular "Great Ideas of Modern Mathematics"
(Dover, $2.00). The best non-technical survey of post-Einstein attempts to
answer perhaps unanswerable questions of origin, age of Universe, possibility
of life on other worlds, etc. Fundamental theories of cosmology and cosmogony
recounted, explained, evaluated in light of most recent data: Einstein's concepts of relativity, space-time; Milne's a priori world-system; astrophysical
theories of Jeans, Eddington; Hoyle's "continuous creation;" contributions of
dozens more scientists. A faithful, comprehensive critical summary of complex
material presented in an extremely well-written text intended for laymen.
Original publication. Index. xii + 276pp. 5⅜ x 8½. Paperbound $2.00

THE RESTLESS UNIVERSE, Max Born
A remarkably lucid account by a Nobel Laureate of recent theories of wave
mechanics, behavior of gases, electrons and ions, waves and particles, electronic
structure of the atom, nuclear physics, and similar topics. "Much more thorough
and deeper than most attempts . . . easy and delightful," Chemical and Engineer-
ing News. Special feature: 7 animated sequences of 60 figures each showing
such phenomena as gas molecules in motion, the scattering of alpha particles,
etc. 11 full-page plates of photographs. Total of nearly 600 illustrations.
351pp. 6⅛ x 9¼. Paperbound $2.00

PLANETS, STARS AND GALAXIES: DESCRIPTIVE ASTRONOMY FOR BEGINNERS,
A. E. Fanning
What causes the progression of the seasons? Phases of the moon? The Aurora
Borealis? How much does the sun weigh? What are the chances of life on our
sister planets? Absorbing introduction to astronomy, incorporating the latest
discoveries and theories: the solar wind, the surface temperature of Venus, the
pock-marked face of Mars, quasars, and much more. Places you on the frontiers
of one of the most vital sciences of our time. Revised (1966). Introduction by
Donald H. Menzel, Harvard University. References. Index. 45 illustrations.
189pp. 5¼ x 8¼. Paperbound $1.50

GREAT IDEAS IN INFORMATION THEORY, LANGUAGE AND CYBERNETICS,
Jagjit Singh
Non-mathematical, but profound study of information, language, the codes
used by men and machines to communicate, the principles of analog and
digital computers, work of McCulloch, Pitts, von Neumann, Turing, and
Uttley, correspondences between intricate mechanical network of "thinking
machines" and more intricate neurophysiological mechanism of human brain.
Indexes. 118 figures. 50 tables. ix + 338pp. 5⅜ x 8½. Paperbound $2.00

THE MUSIC OF THE SPHERES: THE MATERIAL UNIVERSE — FROM ATOM TO QUASAR, SIMPLY EXPLAINED, *Guy Murchie*
Vast compendium of fact, modern concept and theory, observed and calculated data, historical background guides intelligent layman through the material universe. Brilliant exposition of earth's construction, explanations for moon's craters, atmospheric components of Venus and Mars (with data from recent fly-by's), sun spots, sequences of star birth and death, neighboring galaxies, contributions of Galileo, Tycho Brahe, Kepler, etc.; and (Vol. 2) construction of the atom (describing newly discovered sigma and xi subatomic particles), theories of sound, color and light, space and time, including relativity theory, quantum theory, wave theory, probability theory, work of Newton, Maxwell, Faraday, Einstein, de Broglie, etc. "Best presentation yet offered to the intelligent general reader," *Saturday Review*. Revised (1967). Index. 319 illustrations by the author. Total of xx + 644pp. 5⅜ x 8½.

Vol. 1 Paperbound $2.00, Vol. 2 Paperbound $2.00,
The set $4.00

FOUR LECTURES ON RELATIVITY AND SPACE, *Charles Proteus Steinmetz*
Lecture series, given by great mathematician and electrical engineer, generally considered one of the best popular-level expositions of special and general relativity theories and related questions. Steinmetz translates complex mathematical reasoning into language accessible to laymen through analogy, example and comparison. Among topics covered are relativity of motion, location, time; of mass; acceleration; 4-dimensional time-space; geometry of the gravitational field; curvature and bending of space; non-Euclidean geometry. Index. 40 illustrations. x + 142pp. 5⅜ x 8½.

Paperbound $1.35

HOW TO KNOW THE WILD FLOWERS, *Mrs. William Starr Dana*
Classic nature book that has introduced thousands to wonders of American wild flowers. Color-season principle of organization is easy to use, even by those with no botanical training, and the genial, refreshing discussions of history, folklore, uses of over 1,000 native and escape flowers, foliage plants are informative as well as fun to read. Over 170 full-page plates, collected from several editions, may be colored in to make permanent records of finds. Revised to conform with 1950 edition of Gray's Manual of Botany. xlii + 438pp. 5⅜ x 8½.

Paperbound $2.00

MANUAL OF THE TREES OF NORTH AMERICA, *Charles Sprague Sargent*
Still unsurpassed as most comprehensive, reliable study of North American tree characteristics, precise locations and distribution. By dean of American dendrologists. Every tree native to U.S., Canada, Alaska; 185 genera, 717 species, described in detail—leaves, flowers, fruit, winterbuds, bark, wood, growth habits, etc. plus discussion of varieties and local variants, immaturity variations. Over 100 keys, including unusual 11-page analytical key to genera, aid in identification. 783 clear illustrations of flowers, fruit, leaves. An unmatched permanent reference work for all nature lovers. Second enlarged (1926) edition. Synopsis of families. Analytical key to genera. Glossary of technical terms. Index. 783 illustrations, 1 map. Total of 982pp. 5⅜ x 8.

Vol. 1 Paperbound $2.25, Vol. 2 Paperbound $2.25,
The set $4.50

TREES OF THE EASTERN AND CENTRAL UNITED STATES AND CANADA,
W. M. Harlow
A revised edition of a standard middle-level guide to native trees and important escapes. More than 140 trees are described in detail, and illustrated with more than 600 drawings and photographs. Supplementary keys will enable the careful reader to identify almost any tree he might encounter. xiii + 288pp. 5⅜ x 8.   Paperbound $1.45

INSECT LIFE AND INSECT NATURAL HISTORY, *S. W. Frost*
A work emphasizing habits, social life, and ecological relations of insects, rather than more academic aspects of classification and morphology. Prof. Frost's enthusiasm and knowledge are everywhere evident as he discusses insect associations and specialized habits like leaf-rolling, leaf-mining, and case-making, the gall insects, the boring insects, aquatic insects, etc. He examines all sorts of matters not usually covered in general works such as: insects as human food, insect music and musicians, insect response to electric and radio waves, use of insects in art and literature. The admirably executed purpose of this book, which covers the middle ground between elementary treatment and scholarly monographs, is to excite the reader to observe for himself. Over 700 illustrations. Extensive bibliography. x + 542pp. 5⅜ x 8.   Paperbound $2.50

HANDBOOK OF BIRDS OF EASTERN NORTH AMERICA,
Frank M. Chapman
Formerly *the* field guide to Eastern birds. Still contains most complete descriptions of plumages, behavior, nest and eggs, habitat, etc. as observed in the field by Chapman and other important ornithologists. Generally, the most comprehensive compendium of bird lore available in the handbook format. Color keys. Illustrated synopsis of orders and suborders. Index. 195 illustrations. xxxvi + 581pp. 5⅜ x 8½.   Paperbound $3.25

LIFE HISTORIES OF NORTH AMERICAN BIRDS, *Arthur Cleveland Bent*
Monumental series of books on North American birds, prepared and published under auspices of Smithsonian Institution. The definitive coverage of the subject; the most-used single source of information. Entire 22-volume set now available from Dover in inexpensive paperbound format. An encyclopedic collection of detailed, specific observations utilizing reports of hundreds of contemporary observers, writings of such naturalists as Audubon, Burroughs, William Brewster, as well as author's own extensive investigations. Contains literally everything known about life history of each bird considered (over 1160 species): nesting, eggs, plumage, distribution and migration, voice, enemies, courtship display, etc. Each volume fully illustrated with up to 393 photographs.   22-volume complete set, Paperbound $59.95

Prices subject to change without notice.

Available at your book dealer or write for free catalogue to Dept. Adsci, Dover Publications, Inc., 180 Varick St., N.Y., N.Y. 10014. Dover publishes more than 150 books each year on science, elementary and advanced mathematics, biology, music, art, literary history, social sciences and other areas.